The Mystery of Esther

The Mystery of Esther

Frank J. Olsen
with Larry Pileggi
and Faith Reynolds

Companion Press
P.O. Box 310
Shippensburg, PA 17257

"Good Stewards of the
Manifold Grace of God"

ISBN 1-56043-633-6

For Worldwide Distribution
Printed in the U.S.A.

Acknowledgments

How did this all come about? Back in 1990 while working my carpentry job at the home of Larry and Jeanette Pileggi, a conversation began on the topic of the Book of Esther. I can still recall some of the remarks we made about the heroine, villain, and the deliverance mentioned in the story. But was that the whole story? From my knowledge of the rest of the Scriptures, I clearly saw and understood that the Holy Scriptures never could have been the product of human intelligence. It was quite obvious that a collection of writings from a time frame so large and involving so many penmen could not be the product of coincidence. Its divine inspiration also speaks profoundly through the material and the information that it contains. Thus with this knowledge and concept, I always believed that the mind of God had reasons and purposes beyond the heroine, villain, and deliverance themes that are recorded in the Book of Esther. Besides, the last chapter of Esther declares that the information recorded in it had been taken from the existing Persian chronicles.

Larry and I continued conversing on the subject. As we did, information and insights began coming my way and ideas started surfacing. After a number of months of these discussions, I remember making this remark: "Larry, there is something more here than just isolated themes and truths." It was as if our findings had to be and could only be told in book form. Thus after many conversations and notations, a rough manuscript was formed. So far two years had passed. At this stage, I again was involved in construction. This time I was working on the residence of a lady named Faith Reynolds. Again the topic of Esther came into our conversation, but this time in regard to what I had been doing. After revealing that I was writing a book, I stated that I could sure use some help. Upon hearing this, Faith, a high school English teacher, volunteered her time and abilities.

Thus both Larry and Faith have been "prime-time" in this endeavor. Numerous other people also have been involved, along with many authors who have influenced my thoughts and helped supply the basis of this writing. I believe it was the inspiration of God that gave me the insight of Esther as a drama. Although criticisms and verdicts will come, the satisfaction that someone might be enlightened and blessed is more than sufficient.

I also want to thank two wives, my wife Birgitta and Larry's wife Jeanette, who had to relinquish much time from their lives to allow us to work on this project, as well as Kim and Steven Pileggi, two children who otherwise could have had some good times with their dad. Only eternity will reveal what those sacrifices have accomplished. I also want to mention my son-in-law, Rev. Leonard Maglione, who did much computer work and was a constant sounding board, whether the time was convenient or not. Others to whom I want to give my appreciation include Rev. Mike Troiano, pastor of Church of The Harvest, Riverhead, New York; Kurt Reimann, Professor at Suffolk Community College and a Bible teacher at Smithtown Gospel Tabernacle in Smithtown, New York; Kit Farrell, Pastoral Secretary, Smithtown Gospel Tabernacle; Madelyn Sendlewski, Chairperson of Suffolk County Christian Coalition; Danny Oliver, a technical writer for Reuters Intl.; and Diane Vitale with NYNEX, Directory Assistance Bureau. All these people were willing to read and give constructive criticism. I especially want to thank Diane Vitale who not only aided me with her reading of the manuscript and giving me her insights and criticisms, but also encouraged me to keep going when I needed that encouragement.

This is one of these times in life when the best of languages seems to be lacking for words, so I thank you one and all.

Frank J. Olsen

Contents

Foreword

Both history and science, if viewed with an honest heart, provide an abundance of evidence that reveal the activity of a divine Creator and Sustainer of life. God, who has revealed Himself in nature, has also provided a means for any seeker of truth to secure an accurate understanding of His character, purpose, and plan for mankind. His Word, the Holy Bible, stands as a lamp that sheds light on all of His handiwork.

The Bible is a historical book that reveals the hand of a God who is involved in the affairs of all people. It also shows that there are people with whom He is intimately involved. The Bible is a prophetic book as well, one that discloses many things intended to direct and help people make proper preparations for what lies ahead.

Within the pages of this divinely inspired manuscript lies a book entitled Esther. For many readers, the Book of Esther is often overlooked, considered insignificant or irrelevant to the body of information gathered from the rest of the Scriptures. The author presents in this work a shining light of truth, revealing a prophetic voice emanating from the Book of Esther. The fingerprint of God is clearly seen unveiling His activity on behalf of His people. A prophetic voice rings out, proclaiming the timeless nature and plans of the living God throughout history and extending into the realm of eternity.

This book provides a thought-provoking, inspiring look at the Book of Esther and the living God who desires to be discovered as a God who can always be found dwelling in the midst of His people.

Pastor Mike Troiano
Church of The Harvest
Riverhead, New York

Preface

Has God concealed in the pages of the Book of Esther the past, present, and future of both the Jews and His Church? With remarkable insight and profound understanding of the Scriptures, the author, in unmasking each character in Esther, adds a provocative new dimension to this already beautiful and inspiring story.

With marvelous historical corroboration, the author traces God's dealings, His plans, and His purposes for Israel (His chosen people) and His Church (those who have accepted His Son). In faithfully proceeding with the story line, he provides the reader with a rare and intriguing prophetic glimpse at some of the past, present, and final future acts in the story of history as we know it.

Kurt W. Reimann, Professor
Suffolk County Community College
Long Island, New York

Bible Teacher
Smithtown Gospel Tabernacle
Smithtown, New York

Introduction

Esther is one of the most overlooked books in the Old Testament. Some people question the validity of its inclusion in the Holy Scriptures and still others have simply neglected to read it. This book will shed light on some fascinating correlations between the individuals and their plights as recorded in the Book of Esther in both Jewish and Christian Bibles. We will view these parallels in light of other Scriptures with regard to past history, current events, and the prophetic future.

It is very important to read the Book of Esther in the Holy Scriptures before reading this book. After the prerequisite reading has been met, we also suggest keeping biblical Esther on hand as you journey through *The Mystery of Esther.*

Esther will be viewed as a drama with every person acting out his/her part as the prophetic script unfolds. The story lines, conflicts, and final resolution will take on immense importance as we see Esther, not only historically, but also as a drama that portrays the final curtain of history. God's Holy Word can be compared to one gigantic, flawless mosaic. Each tile of this work of art represents a scribe, called and inspired by the Holy Spirit to contribute to the larger picture.

Moses was proclaimed to be learned in all of the sciences of his day. He was a highly qualified teacher and he penned his books (the Pentateuch) from that perspective. David, the sweet singer of Israel, penned his inspired Psalms in a poetic style yet to be equaled. Matthew, Mark, Luke, and John were witnesses of their day who obeyed God and gave us their inspired, yet personal, views in the Gospels. Paul, who perhaps perceived God's plan far better than anyone else of his day, "presents his case" in his letters.

The writer of Esther could have been inspired and chosen by God as a "playwright" to present this most exciting drama. Perhaps this drama is being played out before the witnesses of history's last throes. Why not?

We want the reader to examine Esther and the amazing parallels of past history and modern-day events. In this examination we want the reader to clearly see that this is not merely coincidence, but that Almighty God, in His wisdom, has allowed these revelations "for such a time as this."

Not all readers hold to the same premise. However, the following 14 basic tenets establish points that are essential to the understanding of this drama's unfolding message.

1. There is one sovereign God in a triune Godhead: Father, Son, and Holy Spirit. Each member of the Godhead plays an independent, yet harmonized role.

2. God has a sevenfold spiritual nature as described in Isaiah 11:2.

   This nature includes the following:

   The Spirit of His Presence

   The Spirit of Wisdom

The Spirit of Understanding

The Spirit of Counsel

The Spirit of Might

The Spirit of Knowledge

The Spirit of the Fear (reverential respect) of the Lord (who is a consuming fire)

3. God's plan was to create a nation to bring forth the Savior for the world. God is calling forth a people unto Himself through this Savior.

4. There is a literal nation, a group of people called "Israel." Scripture outlines her origins (Gen. 12:1-2), calling (Is. 48:12-17), failures (Deut. 18:18-19), repentance (Zech. 13:9), and ultimate glorious destiny (Deut. 28:1-14).

5. There is a nation outlined in the New Testament called "The Church." Scripture outlines her origins (Acts 2:1-4), calling (1 Pet. 2:9), and ultimate glorious destiny (Rev. 20:6).

6. Scripture informs us that there has been a rebellion against God by angelic (Rev. 12:7) as well as human beings (Is. 1:2) led by the fallen archangel (Gen. 3:1) (lucifer, satan, devil).

7. There is a continual war waging between the god of this world (satan) and the true God revealed in Holy Scriptures (Is. 14:13-14).

8. John 1:1 declares the Eternal Word. John 1:14 declares that the Eternal Word became the Living Word (Jesus, Emmanuel). The Old Testament heralds Him to be Prophet, Priest, and King. In the past He was (that

Prophet), today He is (the High Priest), and for the near future He will be (the King).

9. Satan's agenda is to destroy the Messianic bloodline (spiritually and physically) to try to annul God's plan by cutting off the Messiah and destroying the only hope of mankind, to keep mankind separated from the true God (Rev. 12:7-13).

10. Satan will masquerade as the true light to accomplish his diabolical goals (2 Cor. 11:14).

11. In the end times (or last days) there will be a self-willed king who will rule a ten-nation confederacy (Dan. 7:19-28).

12. Scripture reveals that a being has been planning for total control of the earth. In the end, however, his maneuverings to become absolute ruler over the earth will fail, and the earth will be handed over to a much more qualified individual (Rev. 13:1-8).

13. Scriptures reveal the crowning of a King by a host of others who have been crowned themselves (Rev. 4:1-11; 19:11-13).

14. There will be a catching away of God's saints, an event commonly referred to as the Rapture (1 Thess. 4:16-17).

It will be interesting to note how these truths are dramatized in the account of Esther. Keep in mind that the Book of Esther depicts real people in real events. On another level, however, these real people are actors in a drama created and inspired by God. They are acting out past, present, and future events as illustrated in the Bible.

The General Outline

1. Esther 1:1–2:23

   Intrigues of Ahasuerus' court of Shushan.

2. Esther 3:1–5:14

   Haman's plot against the Jews.

3. Esther 6:1–10:3

   The victory of the Jews.

The Setting

1. *The Great Persian Empire*, symbolic of God's earthly domain.

2. *Shushan*, the capital city of King Ahasuerus, literally translated "lily."

3. *Babylon,* literally translated "a place of confusion." Symbolic of the whole earth.

Historical Background and Summary

Even though God's name is never mentioned in the Book of Esther,[1] throughout the book it is evident that the hand of God is at work on behalf of His people.

Ahasuerus' wife, Vashti, refuses to make a public appearance before the princes and the nobles in the king's court. She is removed from her position as queen and Esther, her successor, is chosen. Later, Haman is angered over the refusal of Mordecai to bow before him and he plans to massacre all the Jews. The king agrees to this.

When Mordecai learns about the plot, he seeks Esther's help,[2] and asks her to intercede with the king. She chooses the path of possibility and enters the inner court of the king's presence without being summoned. After a favorable reception, she arranges a first and second banquet with the king, herself, and Haman. Prior to these events, Mordecai had discovered a plot against the king's life. At that time he reported it through Esther and the assassins were apprehended and executed. Meanwhile, Mordecai had gone unrewarded. Then the king, during a restless night, was made aware of this oversight and contemplated a just reward for Mordecai's loyal service.

As the story reaches its climax, Haman gains the king's unchanging commitment to execute all Jews. When Haman hears his plot disclosed to Ahasuerus by Esther, he tries to win her favor after an angry king has left the room. The king, upon his return, finds Haman on the couch of his queen and interprets it as an assault upon his wife. He orders Haman to be hanged on the gallows prepared for Mordecai. Mordecai now takes over the vacated position of Haman.

Since the king's edict cannot be annulled, orders are given for the Jews to defend themselves when the day of reckoning comes. The Jews successfully defend themselves and Mordecai advances, second only to King Ahasuerus in power and position. Mordecai is described in Esther 10:3 as being very great among the Jews. Respected by all his countrymen, he did his best for his people. He was a friend at court for all of them. Finally, the Feast of Purim is instituted as a reminder of God's great deliverance of His people (see Lindell Study Bible, The Living Bible, p. 587).

It is of utmost importance to be familiar with and to understand the characters and the roles they play in this drama. They are listed in the following charts.

PROGRAM OF PLAYERS

Character Description / Role—and Prophetic Symbol of Each [3]

Name:	Meaning:	Role:	Verse:
Ahasuerus GK: Xerxes	The Venerable King Ruler of Heroic Men	Eternal Sovereign King of Universe (Adonai)	1:1
Vashti	One Who Is Desired	Israel	1:9
Hegai	My Meditations (Silent Worker)	God—The Holy Spirit (As Administrator)	2:3
Mordecai	Diety of Mars	God—The Son (The Living Word)	2:5
Jeconiah	Yahweh Establishes	The Disobedient Led Into Captivity	2:6
Nebuchadnezzar	Oh, God Nebo, Protect My Son	Satan: Beginning of the Gentile System of Governments	2:6
Esther (Per.) Hadassah (Heb.)	Star, Brilliance, Light Myrtle (Fragrance, Preservative)	The Church: All Those Born of God's Spirit	2:7
Shaashgaz	Lover of Beauty (Superficial)	Overseer of False Religion	2:14
Abihail	Father of Might	God—The Father (The Almighty)	2:15
Bigthan	Gift of God	False Spiritual Ideology	2:21
Teresh	Solid	False Political Ideology	2:21
Haman	Literally Means "Splendid" (However, it sounds like a Hebrew word for "commotion.")	Antichrist: The Personification of Evil	3:1
Hathach	Good	God—The Holy Spirit (As Communicator)	4:5
Zeresh	A Stranger in Want	A False Prophet	5:10

Name:	Meaning:	Role:	Verse:
Ahasuerus' (Xerxes) seven servants			
Mehuman Biztha Harbana Bigtha Abagtha Zethar Carcas	Trusty Bound Donkey Driver/ Chauffeur Gift of God Happy/Prosperous Conqueror Vulture	This group of seven represents the seven spirits listed in Isaiah 11:2. They represent attributes necessary for executive power.	1:10
Ahasuerus' (Xerxes) seven wise men			
Carshena Shethat Admatha Tarshish Meres Marsena Memucan	Plowman Commander Unconquered Yellow Jasper Forgetful One Forgetful Man Sorcerer	This group of seven represents the seven spirits listed in Isaiah 11:2. They represent attributes necessary for judicial/legislative power.	1:14
Esther's seven maidens			
		This group of seven represents the seven spirits listed in Isaiah 11:2. They represent attributes necessary for administrative power.	2:9

The above three groups of sevens will portray four aspects necessary for any type of government to function. They constitute the executive, judicial, legislative, and administrative branches.

Name:	Meaning:	Role:	Verse:
Haman's ten sons			
Parshandatha	Inquisitive (Knowledge)	The names of	9:7
Dalphon	The Weeper (The Loser)	Haman's ten sons all	
Aspatha	The Enticed Gathered	relate to the origin	
Poratha	Bounteous (Wealth)	and characteristics	
Adalia	Meaning Unknown	of Haman.	
Parmashta	Strong Fisted (Might)		
Arisai	Meaning Unknown		
Aridatha	Given by Hari*		
Aridai	Delight of Hari*		
Vajezatha	Son of the Atmosphere ("Prince of the Power of the Air")		
*Hari can be translated as "god."			

Are there truths in the Book of Esther that are relevant for us today? Does God have a message that He has chosen to reveal, only now, in these last days? Could the revelation of Esther be God's final instruction to His people?

Are you and I part of *His people,* the people for whom the King is coming? A close examination of this book will provide some provocative challenges for you. You are about to begin a prophetic odyssey with God's Holy Word as a foundation. Let the "drama" of Esther commence.

End Notes

1. God is omnipresent and, therefore, is everywhere. There are times, however, that God will "...surely hide His face..." (Deut. 31:18). God's name is not *specifically* mentioned in Esther, but His almighty presence and sovereignty reign.

2. Please take note of the emphasis for future reference in later chapters as the prophetic symbolism, specifically as the activities of Esther and Mordecai, become manifest.

3. The comprehension of this character description chart is absolutely necessary if the prophetic scenario that follows is to be understood. The reader will need to constantly refer to these pages. Kindly mark these pages for future reference. They will serve as program notes for this drama.

Chapter 1

Glory and Grief in the Kingdom

An unbroken thread runs throughout Holy Scripture, from the call of Abraham in Genesis to the last book of the Old Testament, Malachi. It reveals an awesome, almighty God calling forth a nation, a people for Himself.

God continues to promise, prophetically declare, and supernaturally work to draw a people to Himself. He began this task thousands of years ago. Israel's glories and destinies, dispersions and regatherings were foretold by the prophets. Surrounding nations were confronted with the unique relationship of Israel and her God, a relationship marked by mighty wonders.

Enemy efforts to sabotage the unveiling of Israel's glories have been and will continue to be countered. God has declared that He shall accomplish His ultimate purposes. The Book of Esther provides us with a vignette of God's working within human history to fulfill His covenant promises.

Conventions: Their Purposes

Esther 1:1-9

The drama begins with Ahasuerus, the king of Persia. In the third year of his reign, he calls his nobles and princes to his capital city to hold a leadership convention. His intention is, through an awesome display of his riches and power, to establish in the minds of everyone present the vast extent of his honor and glory.

These princes and nobles have already shown their love and loyalty for the king, even to the extent of risking their lives in the battles to expand his empire. Truly the strength of his empire is built upon what his Greek name, *Xerxes*, implies: "ruler of heroic men."

The king is hosting the convention in this way so the greatness of the king's kingdom will filter back to all of the inhabitants of his empire. Each prince and noble will return to his respective province with glorious reports. Ahasuerus, the king of Persia, will take 180 days to make these glories known.

In like fashion, the King of the Universe, God or *Adonai* in the Hebrew language, began calling His representatives in the third millennia of time. He wanted to reveal His riches, power, and glory to all mankind. First, He called a man named Abram. Abram means "exalted father." Abram was childless when God changed his name to Abraham, meaning "father of a multitude," and made a covenant with him.

Abraham is known for his wealth and leadership, but his primary hallmark is obedience to God. Called from his native residence, Abraham obeyed. God directed Abraham to travel to a particular place. There He promised him a specific land and established a covenant with him.

This covenant, initiated with Abraham, was also witnessed and confirmed with Isaac, his son, and Jacob, his grandson. A new nation, Israel, was established, and this Israel is characterized in Scripture as, among other things, "God's wife." The land, at first called Canaan, later became known as the land of Israel. This segment of earth became God's selected earthly headquarters.

The name *Shushan* plays two symbolic roles. "Shushan the palace" portrays the city of Jerusalem while "Shushan the city" symbolizes the whole land of Israel. The earliest meaning of Shushan's root word is "exalt" or "rejoice." Israel is the place where God's Person and Will were initially revealed and Israel has been directly affiliated with this ever since. Even so, Jerusalem and Israel will become exalted and be a place of rejoicing when the rightful King appears.

Israel's capital city, Jerusalem, is symbolized in Esther by the king's palace. It was the seat of the king's power in Persia. Jerusalem is where the King of the Universe (Adonai) will ultimately reveal His power and glory. The heavenly Ruler wanted to reveal His nature through a people. Here, in Jerusalem, God broadcasted an initial request for a people to come to the forefront. This request was based upon His character of holiness, justice, and love.

His holiness distinguishes His Word from all other writings. Because of His justice, He must and does make correct judgments. Because of His love, His judgments are tempered, and He makes merciful provisions.

Israel multiplied through Jacob. God continued to call and utilize His leaders: Moses, Joshua, the judges, the kings, the prophets, and the priests. The number of His earthly representatives grew and all of the inhabitants of the earth heard and saw the riches and power of their heavenly King. He made Himself known through the words and actions of His servants in Israel. The King of the Universe (Adonai) took approximately 1,500 years to make known, not only His riches and power, but also His future plans and promises. Ahasuerus, the king of Persia, took a mere 180 days to make his glories known.

A Costly and Regrettable Decision

Esther 1:9-22

As a grand finale to his 180-day convention, the king of Persia is hosting a week-long feast. This feast is to conclude on the seventh day with a display of the queen's beauty, the crowning glory of all that the king is and all that he possesses.

After displaying his vast kingdom and power, he plans to display his beautiful bride, Vashti, his first love. The queen is to present herself, wearing the crown (an ornament that sets her apart from all the other women in the kingdom). The king sends his seven servants to summon Vashti to present herself before him, the leaders, and all the people who are present in Shushan—the palace.

Vashti fails to make her appearance and, instead of a glorious climax, the very fiber of the kingdom is challenged. Only righteous decisions and quick actions will prevent setting the wheels of anarchy in motion. Failure to obey any orders issued by the king is an absolute violation of Persian law. Justice has to reign. The wise men make a decision to demote Vashti from her elevated position. The king ratifies their decision. His seven wise men suggest that the king consider looking for another queen. Upholding their judgment, the king authorizes these wise men to implement their decision. Immediately, dispatches are sent throughout the kingdom in search of a candidate to fill the vacated position.

In a similar fashion, God, the righteous King, took hundreds of years to progressively reveal Himself. He called forth His chosen leaders from Israel. He called this nation "His wife." He wanted her to represent His crowning glory. Just as Vashti, whose name means "to be desired," was desired by her king, God desired Israel. He wanted her to appear before the nations of earth wearing a crown of righteousness, faith, and obedience as a revelation of Himself, a just and loving God.

Vashti, Ahasuerus' queen, embroiled in hostessing a banquet for the wives of the nobles and princes, was no doubt the center of attraction. Captivated by this attention, she placed her immediate activities above the king's command and failed to respond to his orders. In the same way, a lot of religious activity and tradition have been more important to Israel than a serene relationship with her eternal King.

Busily involved with her role, Israel, like Vashti, failed to heed the seven servants sent with orders from her King. The role of the seven servants corresponds to the seven aspects of the Spirit of God, listed in Isaiah 11:1-2.

1. The Spirit of His Presence

2. The Spirit of Wisdom

3. The Spirit of Understanding

4. The Spirit of Counsel

5. The Spirit of Might

6. The Spirit of Knowledge

7. The Spirit of the Fear (reverential respect) of the Lord

According to Professor Edwin M. Yamauchi's book *Persia and the Bible*, the demotion of a queen did take place during this time period. (He also mentions how she again resurfaces to a position of power at a later date.)

The Spirit of the Lord spoke through Moses in Deuteronomy.

Behold, I set before you this day a blessing and a curse; a blessing, if ye obey the commandments of the Lord your God, which I command you this day: and a curse, if ye will not obey the commandments of the Lord your God, but turn aside out of the way which I command you this day, to go after other gods, which ye have not known (Deuteronomy 11:26-28).

The Lord thy God will raise up unto thee a Prophet from the midst of thee [Israel] of thy brethren, like unto me [Moses]; unto him ye shall hearken (Deuteronomy 18:15).

I will raise them [Israel] up a Prophet from among their brethren, like unto thee [Moses], and will put My words in his mouth; and he shall speak unto them all that I shall command him. And it shall come to pass, that whosoever will not hearken unto My words which he shall speak in My name, I will require it of him (Deuteronomy 18:18-19).

Indirectly, these Scriptures reveal that the sevenfold Spirit of God would rest upon a Prophet to come. Surely the seven spiritual characteristics (previously listed) were witnessed in the life of Moses. There are more than 300 direct references in the Old Testament that give specific information regarding that particular Prophet of Deuteronomy

18:15. The description found in Isaiah 11:1 is especially pertinent for this study of the Book of Esther: "And there shall come forth a rod out of the stem of Jesse, and a Branch shall grow out of his roots." He would be a person from the genealogy of Judah and from the house of David.

The genealogy in the Gospel of Matthew declares that the person who fulfills Isaiah's description is Jesus. Beginning with His baptism (when the Presence of God's Spirit descended upon Him), the Gospels continually bear witness that Jesus was led by the Spirit and manifested the sevenfold descriptive aspects. Matthew 3:16 states, "And Jesus, when He was baptized, went up straightway out of the water: and, lo, the heavens were opened unto him [John the Baptist], and he saw the Spirit of God descending like a dove, and lighting upon Him."

This visible confirmation of the Spirit of God in the life of Jesus kept reoccurring. Another instance, recorded in Matthew 17:2, observes: "And [Jesus] was transfigured before them: and His face did shine as the sun and His raiment was white as the light." This parallels Moses' experience at Mount Sinai when his face shone after spending 40 days with the Spirit of the Presence of God. (See Exodus 34:30.)

In addition to the visual aspect, the Spirit of Knowledge and the Spirit of Wisdom were continuously observed in the life of Jesus. One typical situation involved the Pharisees and Herodians, two religious sects who tried to entrap Jesus. Mark 12:14-17 describes the exchange:

And when they were come, they say unto Him, Master, we know that Thou art true, and carest for no man: for Thou regardest not the person of men, but teachest the way of God in truth: Is it lawful to give tribute to Caesar, or not? Shall we give, or shall we not give? But He, knowing their hypocrisy, said unto them, Why tempt ye Me? bring Me a penny, that I may see it.... [When they had done so and had, in response to Jesus' questioning, identified the image on it as Caesar's, Jesus pointedly stated:] *Render to Caesar the things that are Caesar's and to God the things that are God's. And they marvelled at Him* (Mark 12:14-17).

This incident closes with Mark's observation: "And they marvelled at Him," the usual response of humanity to the Spirit of Wisdom and the Spirit of Knowledge. Jesus brought these into their lives and presented them with opportunities to understand.

In John 5:14 Jesus let it be known that sin does play a direct part in affliction: "Afterward Jesus findeth him [the impotent man whom He had healed by the sheep market pool] in the temple, and said unto him, Behold, thou art made whole: sin no more, lest a worse thing come unto thee." The impact of the Spirit of Knowledge and the Spirit of Wisdom in the life of Jesus, along with the Spirit of Understanding, is summarized by Luke 2:47: "And all that heard Him were astonished at His understanding and answers."

The Spirit of Might incorporates a wide range of powers, from that of the master chemist (turning water into wine at the wedding in Cana), to the greatest physicist, in absolute control of the laws of nature (walking on the turbulent Sea of Galilee and calming the violent storm). Further, His visit to Lazarus' tomb demonstrated that the power of life within

Jesus annulled the power of death. Lazarus, dead for three days, returned to life at the command of Jesus. To the demoniac who lived in a cemetery because his torments restricted him from a life of freedom and normalcy, Jesus brought freedom. The mightiest of His works, His own resurrection, Jesus foretold in John 10:17: "Therefore doth My Father love Me, because I lay down My life, that I might take it again."

The last of the seven attributes, the Spirit of the Fear of the Lord, is defined as "awed, reverential respect." It is a respect that comes from the clear knowledge that, in the face of rebellion and sin, God is an all-consuming fire. Hell is a real place created by God for all who participate in sin and rebellion. Jesus manifested reverential respect in every facet of His life. In His ministry, He always deferred to and honored His Father in word and deed. He demonstrated what it means to "love the Lord thy God with all thy heart" (Mk. 12:30) by His life.

Israel's leadership, both civil and religious, did not recognize this Prophet and His message. They considered His identification with God as blasphemous. Scriptures clearly defined this Prophet "like unto Moses" (see Deut. 18:15) and declared the utmost importance of His message.

She (Israel), the beautiful wife of the King of the Universe, was to reflect all that He was in splendor and majesty to the world. She refused to hear His voice and to be the vehicle to display His glory. The King's primary expectation was obedience. Both Vashti, the wife of Ahasuerus, and Israel were lax in exhibiting this quality.

The Spirit of God cannot violate man's free will. He works to usher man into the presence of God, just as King Ahasuerus' servants planned to do for Queen Vashti. John 1:10-11 declares, "He was in the world, and the world was made by Him, and the world knew Him not. He came unto His own, and His own received Him not."

The servants of the king of Persia took a message to the king's wife. Also, the Spirit of God, working through Jesus the Living Word (filled with the sevenfold nature of God), went to Israel with a message. This message commissioned her to come into the presence of God for the specific purpose of revealing His glory to mankind. Just as Vashti failed to respond to the king's command, Israel failed to respond to God's invitation. In this we witness a parallel between the executive orders of both sovereigns and corresponding violations.

King Ahasuerus, after hearing and agreeing with the judicious decision from his seven wise men, endorsed their unanimous proposal. A search was set in motion for one to assume the royal estate from which Vashti had been demoted. This account in Esther has a parallel in the parable of the wedding banquet, recorded in Matthew 22:1-14.

And Jesus answered and spake unto them again by parables, and said, The kingdom of heaven is like unto a certain king, which made a marriage for his son, and sent forth his servants to call them that were bidden to the wedding: and they would not come. Again, he sent forth other servants, saying, Tell them which are bidden, Behold, I have prepared my dinner: my oxen and my fatlings are killed, and all things are ready: come unto the marriage. But they made light of it, and went their ways, one to his farm, another to his merchandise: and the remnant took his servants, and entreated them spitefully, and slew them. But when the king heard thereof, he was wroth: and he sent forth his armies, and destroyed those murderers, and burned up their city. Then saith he to his servants, The wedding is ready, but they which were bidden were not worthy. Go ye therefore into the highways, and as many as ye shall find, bid to the marriage. So those servants went out into the highways, and gathered together all as many as they found, both bad and good: and the wedding was furnished with guests. And when the king came in to see the guests, he saw there a man which had not on a wedding garment: and he saith unto him, Friend, how camest thou in hither not having a wedding garment? And he was speechless. Then said the king to the servants, Bind him hand and foot, and take him away, and cast him into outer darkness; there shall be weeping and gnashing of teeth. For many are called, but few are chosen (Matthew 22:1-14).

The specifics of the preceding parable parallel the events of Esther very clearly:

1. The sending forth of servants with a message.

2. The refusal of the message by those to whom it was sent.

3. The anger of the king, a judgment, and an action taken.

4. The message sent by the king has now been sent to new candidates.

5. A positive response to the king's message as recorded in the events of Esther and as illustrated in the wedding banquet parable.

Events in Esther, played out in history, parallel the heavenly King sending His messenger (His Son), symbolized by the seven servants, to His people Israel who, like Queen Vashti of Persia, were to be the king's crowning glory. Israel also refused her King's directive. Israel's failure to obey angered her heavenly King. For this reason His people have been scattered throughout the nations. She has been demoted from the position of a glorified nation among the nations, but not forever.

We can see parallels in the king's messages. There were violations, judgments, and new directives given and implemented. This same message, first delivered to Israel, has been sent to all mankind. This message, the gospel, has been preached to all the nations. For those who respond properly, there will be a final acceptance by the King.

Both the Book of Esther and the Gospels demonstrate that God speaks to mankind through His recorded and prophetic Word. As this Word is fulfilled in history, God uses the power of fulfilled prophecy to convince men to put their faith and trust in Him.

Chapter 2

Justice and Love Fulfilled

The Candidates

Esther 2:1-4

His anger appeased, King Ahasuerus (also known as Xerxes), reflects upon the consequences of Queen Vashti's rejection of his command to appear before him, a refusal for which she had been penalized and demoted from her position. Her negligence in obeying her husband and king was, in essence, a direct assault upon his authority. In addition, he was deprived of one who should have been a visible demonstration of his love and glory. His ministers' suggestion to seek a replacement for Vashti pleased him.

So the king's agents begin an intensive search throughout the empire for candidates. From these the king will choose one to wear the crown. These fair young women are brought to Hegai, the king's chief chamberlain in charge of the women. In this role, Hegai, more than any other, knows the king's preferences and his standards. He is well qualified to act on the king's behalf.

Consider the drama's parallel of King Ahasuerus' situation to the King of the Universe (who has also been grieved). Israel, God's wife, refused to respond to her loving Creator and Ruler. This brought anarchy into His earthly kingdom. A judgment was made and authorization given to search for a new bride. The Holy Spirit of God began the task.

Just as the message to seek a replacement for Vashti was delivered throughout the entire realm of the Persian Empire, the message of the gospel has been sent forth into the whole world. This message is, "Whosoever will, let him come by faith and receive that which God has offered, a garment of righteousness and eternal life." The Holy Spirit is keenly aware of attitudes, especially those of a contrite heart. He also looks for the accompanying attributes of faith and obedience. These are the qualities required to please the heavenly King, qualities that the Holy Spirit (represented by Hegai) is more than qualified to discern. He acts in light of His intimate knowledge of the heavenly Sovereign.

Scripture proclaims the activity of the Holy Spirit after His coming. (See John 16:13.) He will speak nothing of Himself. His work is to recognize the people who will be accepted by the heavenly Sovereign. Before that occurs, however, the Holy Spirit is responsible for providing everything necessary for the final selection. Both the Holy Spirit and Hegai carry out the orders of their sovereigns. In both cases the end result will be satisfactory because both are eminently qualified for the positions they hold.

A Candidate Favored

Esther 2:5-8

Chapter 2 discusses one candidate in particular: Esther. It refers to her nationality, her birth, her upbringing, her father, and one close relative. Her relative, Mordecai, is the central figure. True, Esther's part is important. Because of her the king is pacified, his joy is restored, and his kingdom is preserved. However, Mordecai plays the primary role in this drama as it unfolds. Esther is separated from Mordecai and Hegai is given the responsibility of seeing that her needs are met.

The analogies drawn to this point of the drama are the following: King Ahasuerus represents the King of the Universe (Adonai). The seven servants and seven wise men portray executive and judicial powers in action. They carry out the executive orders, judge the violations, and institute new directives. Hegai parallels the Holy Spirit in the role of the administrator.

Who is this relative called Mordecai? Translated literally his name means "deity of Mars." Mordecai symbolizes Jesus Christ, the Living Word, as described in the New Testament in John 1:1 and John 1:14. Scripture verifies the deity of Jesus and the unfolding drama of Esther plays out this truth.

Only Esther's father, Abihail, and her cousin Mordecai are mentioned. Interestingly, Mordecai's genealogy is traced more carefully, covering four generations. He had been carried away from Israel in the last captivity and is now in Babylon, not in Israel his homeland. Mordecai finds himself in a foreign land because of the infractions of others from his nation. It was not his wrongdoing.

The Gospel of Matthew opens in precisely the same way, tracing the genealogy of Jesus, God's Son. John 3:16 reads, "For God so loved the world, that He gave His only begotten Son, that whosoever believeth in Him should not perish, but have eternal life." Like Mordecai, He was carried away because of the sins of others. Jesus had to leave Heaven and take on the garment of humanity because of the sins of mankind.

Another correlation can be found in Mordecai's changing position of power. As a result of Esther's selection as queen, Mordecai sits in the king's gate. (See Esther 2:19.) Likewise, Jesus the Living Word, sits in an elevated seat of power in the realm of the Sovereign King of the Universe (God/Adonai). Jesus fills a new position because of His atoning sacrifice for the sins of this world. Psalm 110:1 says, "The Lord said unto my Lord: Sit Thou at My right hand, until I make Thine enemies Thy footstool." Hebrews 1:3 says, "Who being the brightness of His glory, and the express image of His person, and upholding all things by the word of His power, when He had by Himself purged our sins, sat down on the right hand of the Majesty on high."

The next parallel concerns Mordecai's rightful place, which should have been in Israel, among his people, not in Babylon. Jesus' rightful place is on earth, resident with His people. Jesus the Son of God, declared to be the Creator of all things, spent time with Adam and Eve. Because of their sins, this intimate relationship came to an end. He was separated from this relationship because of their actions. God now sends Him to earth with a mission and His rightful place is to be with His creation and those who have faith in Him. The people of faith and obedience are His heritage.

Mordecai's relationship to Esther was through a pure ancestral bloodline. Even so, Jesus, born of the Spirit of God, is related to the Church. The Church is born of this same Holy Spirit. The Church consists of the people who have put their faith in the sacrificial blood of Jesus, the Lamb of God, for the remission of their sins. They have received a new spiritual life and have been placed under His custody.

Throughout the New Testament, the Church is illustrated by expressions such as a Shepherd and His flock (Jn. 10:14); a

Redeemer and His redeemed (Lk. 5:9); the Head and the body (Eph. 5:30); and a completed building of stones with its Cornerstone (Eph. 2:19-22; Col. 1:18). Each expression consists of two specific elements that together depict a oneness. This unity describes the Church. Without the Shepherd, the Redeemer, the Head, or the Cornerstone, we have incompleteness.

Another parallel emerges within Mordecai's charge and responsibility to rear Esther. Jesus is the One who has been given absolute custody of everyone who has been given life from His heavenly Father. They are His to watch over, to provide for, to direct, and to protect. Yet people who have received spiritual life are still separated from their Father in Heaven. Esther was separated from her father, Abihail (father of might) and given to Mordecai her guardian. Esther represents the Church (the "called out" ones). She is also now separated from Mordecai and a new person, Hegai, is given the responsibility of seeing that her needs are met.

Custodianship of the Church has been transferred to the Holy Spirit. At the time of His separation, Jesus the Living Word prepared His disciples with the promise that when the Holy Spirit came, He would continue to lead and guide them to truths vital to their existence in this world. (See John 14.)

Esther 2:9-15

Esther, the daughter of Abihail (father of might), now undergoes an extensive purification process and prepares herself for her appearance before the king. Rather than act independently, she selects only those things that Hegai (symbolic of the Holy Spirit) approves as appropriate for her entrance into the king's chambers.

An aspect of the Holy Spirit's work is depicted in Esther's time of preparation. The heavenly King makes the same demand for anyone coming into His presence. Hebrews 9:22 (NIV) states, "...and without the shedding of blood there is no forgiveness for sin."

A holy God cannot tolerate sin. He demands and accepts nothing less than blood as the perfect cleansing agent for sin. God's consistent expectations are seen in the sacrifices of both Abel and Abraham, the high priests offering up sacrifices in the temple, and finally, in the eternal and all-sufficient One, the Lamb of God Himself, Jesus the Christ. First John 1:7 reads, "But if we walk in the light, as He is in the light, we have fellowship one with another, and the blood of Jesus Christ His Son cleanseth us from all sin." Anyone who chooses to believe, and accepts the atoning sacrifice and infallible Word, can be washed eternally clean.

Ephesians 5:26 says, "That He might sanctify and cleanse it [the Church] with the washing of water by the Word." This group, called the Church in Ephesians 5:27, has been given a commitment—that He might present it to Himself a glorious Church, not having spot or wrinkle or any such thing, but that it should be holy and unblemished.

Like Esther, the Church must undergo an intensive purification process. In conjunction with the requirements of purification, seven maidens helped Esther in her preparation. Again, the significance of seven symbolizes the attributes of the sevenfold Spirit of God. Isaiah 11:2 enumerates His character to us when he says the Spirit of the Lord shall rest upon Him with the following:

1. The Spirit of His Presence

2. The Spirit of Wisdom

3. The Spirit of Understanding

4. The Spirit of Counsel

5. The Spirit of Might

6. The Spirit of Knowledge

7. The Spirit of the Fear (reverential respect) of the Lord

These spiritual attributes of God are given to the Church to help her before she can be accepted by the King. In First Corinthians 13 these attributes are classified as "gifts from God." God, in His foreknowledge, knew the Church could not become complete unless she had divine help. He gave her "seven maidens." He gave Himself to the Church so she could be properly groomed and attired. Just as Esther spent much time in preparation, so the Church has been going and continues to go through her purification. Even as Mordecai kept a watchful eye over Esther, so Jesus, the Living Word, keeps a close watch over His Church. He is concerned for her destiny.

The Church, born by the Eternal Father, the God of Might, needs to depend upon the things that God has provided for her: an atoning sacrifice, God's established Word, and the free gifts of God's Spirit. Collectively, this is called "the grace of God."

When these are received in faith (Esther received only those things Hegai provided for her, and she became the one whom the king favored), to the Church (resting solely on what has been provided for her), comes the privilege of God's favor. In fact, Hebrews 4:16 states, "Let us therefore come boldly unto the throne of grace, that we may obtain mercy, and find grace to help in time of need." Further, Ephesians 2:8 states, "For by grace are ye saved through faith; and that not of yourselves: it is the gift of God."

Esther 2:10

Esther's identity has been kept a secret from her own people; "Esther had not shewed her people nor her kindred: for Mordecai had charged her that she should not shew it" (Esther 2:10). Esther knows that her bloodline makes her a Jewess, but the Jewish people are unaware that one of their own is soon to be installed as the queen.

Again we can draw a parallel. The Church is in the King's court, and her entrance into God's presence will be a new experience (called the Rapture), an awesome, near-future occurrence, and one about which Israel is uninformed. The Church and the House of Israel are related in the sense that they are both God's creations. John 1:1-3 (NIV) says, "In the beginning was the Word, and the Word was with God, and the Word was God. He was with God in the beginning. Through Him all things were made; without Him nothing was made that has been made."

Just as Esther kept her Jewish identity secret, so the true identity of the Church, the Bride of Christ, is still hidden from Israel. Esther is a type of the Church. Vashti is a type of Israel.

Although the early Church was basically composed of enlightened or born-again Jews, in time it became primarily the Gentiles who received the good news and believed. As time went on, what started out as the initial Church became known as Christendom, a composite of true and false, or masquerading, believers. In history many actions of ignorant, false, and misguided Christians have created a chasm between the Jews and Christians.

The identity of the true Church and her relationship to Israel has not been made clear to God's covenant people, Israel. The entrance of the Church (the Bride), into the relationship God designed for Israel, is described in John 12:37-43 (NIV).

Even after Jesus had done all these miraculous signs in their [the Jews] presence, they still would not believe in Him. This was to fulfill the word of Isaiah the prophet: "Lord, who has believed our message and to whom has the arm of the Lord been revealed?" For this reason they could not believe, because, as Isaiah says elsewhere: "He has blinded their eyes and deadened their hearts so they can neither see with their eyes nor understand with their hearts nor turn—and I would heal them." Isaiah said this because he saw Jesus' glory and spoke about Him. Yet at the same time many even among the leaders believed in Him. But because of the Pharisees they would not confess their faith for fear they would be put out of the synagogue; for they loved praise from men more than praise from God.

Again, in Romans 11:7-8 (NIV) the writer observes, "What then? What Israel [its leadership] sought so earnestly it did not obtain, but the elect did. The others were hardened, as it is written: 'God gave them a spirit of stupor, eyes so that they could not see and ears so that they could not hear, to this very day.' "

A New Queen Chosen

Esther 2:16-18

Esther is brought into the presence of the king and crowned as the new queen. She brings joy to the heart of the king.

Just as Esther was chosen, the Church has been chosen. As Esther is brought to the king, he releases abundant blessings to the provinces. The Church, too, brings joy to the heart of the heavenly Sovereign. He has released blessings, stemming from His abundant love, power, and unlimited resources, to all mankind. These blessings are revealed through His written Word and they are available to all who will accept them by faith. These promises include the gift of eternal life (most important of all), as well as all the additional provisions that address man's needs on earth (healings, guidance, protection, etc.).

In the beginning man was created by God for His own good pleasure. Because of sin, man no longer functions as God originally created him. Through the gift of eternal life, the Spirit of God reestablishes His relationship with man. Through God's Son, Jesus Christ, man receives the benefits of His grace: freedom from bondage, hope for hopelessness, healing for affliction, blessing instead of cursing, strength for weakness, and joy for sorrow. God has provided the remedy for the miseries of man's sinful nature as well as defeated the purposes of satan. The King of the Universe has released these benefits to all who come by faith and receive them.

We have completed a presentation of four parallels: (a) the power and riches of the king; (b) the role of the seven servants, wise men, and maidens; (c) the disobedience of Vashti; (d) the crowning of the new queen, Esther.

These parallels are so clear that we believe the following events of Esther also have a definite correlation that proceeds in chronological order and foreshadows actual historical events.

The prophetic picture exposed in the drama of Esther can be likened to Nebuchadnezzar's disturbing dream and

Daniel's interpretation, spoken forth as he was enlightened by God. The dream, recorded in Daniel chapter 2, describes a colossal statue of a man made out of gold, silver, brass, and iron.

Daniel's interpretation correlates these metals with the various Gentile kingdoms that would dominate all people for specific time periods. The Book of Daniel clearly reveals which Gentile kingdoms were represented by the first three metals. Gold represented Nebuchadnezzar and the Babylonian Empire. Silver represented Darius and the Median/Persian Empire. Brass represented Alexander and the Greek Empire. God used this prophetic portrait to give mankind information relative to the times of Gentile world dominion. Has God likewise revealed in Esther, for the benefit of men who will accept and believe, some specific events yet to transpire in history?

The drama continues.

A Short-lived Insurrection

Esther 2:19-23

Esther is queen and Mordecai is sitting in a new position of power, the king's gate. Two chamberlains conspire to overthrow the king. Mordecai learns of the plot and informs Esther. She goes to the king in Mordecai's name and the matter is swiftly resolved. These two conspirators are Bigthan and Teresh.

Bigthan means "gift of God" and Teresh means "solid." Bigthan and Teresh typify two areas of man's being: his spiritual nature and his earthly nature. Man needs leadership and guidance in both areas. God has given His laws (Scriptures) for living and functioning in both realms. The Ten

Commandments address these two areas. The first through the fourth commandments pertain to man's relationship to God and the spiritual realm. The last six pertain to man's relationship to man and the earthly realm.

The characters of Bigthan and Teresh typify a conspiracy to challenge God's Kingdom and His laws in these respective areas. Recent history reflects what these two men portray. Communism is an ideology that is contrary to God's laws and designs. God's Word declares man to be a free moral agent, free to make his own choices within the guidelines of His established law.

The Kingdom of God demands a faith in the character of the God. God requires acceptance, as absolute truth, of the teachings within His Kingdom. A comparison of Scripture with communism reveals how this ideology has challenged God's principles.

Scripture states that there is one true God and He alone should be worshiped (Ex. 34:14). Communism states that outside of man there is no God. Scripture says that the fruit of a man's labor should be enjoyed by the one who labored for it (Is. 15:21-23). Communism says that a man exists for the purpose of the state and the state alone. A long list could be assembled to show the declaration of Scripture and the challenge of communism.

In the Book of Esther the challenge to the kingdom was exposed and swiftly resolved. Similarly, communism, which declared war against the biblical God by its atheistic philosophy, became operational in 1921. Active for only 70 years, it ended in 1991—a short span of time in the light of man's history.

Bigthan and Teresh, the two chamberlains, were removed after Mordecai exposed them (through Esther) to the king. Likewise, communism has been dealt with because of the exposure made by Jesus the Living Word to all believers of His Word. These believers have faithfully petitioned the heavenly King, in the name of Jesus (our Mordecai), to judge the anti-God stance of communism.

Communism was a marriage of spiritual and political ideology for the enslavement of man and the overthrow of God's Kingdom and purposes on earth. We can say Darwin (atheism) "married" Marx/Lenin (socialism), or vice versa.

It is interesting that when God called Abraham in 1921 B.C., He began to reveal and establish His Kingdom on earth. His Kingdom was challenged by Soviet communism from A.D. 1921 through A.D. 1991. The King of the Universe dealt communism a swift and fatal blow. In the light of God and eternity, or even time as we know it, it was a short-lived challenge.

Chapter 3

Conspiracy at a High Level

Esther chapter 3 begins with, "After these things...." This phrase reveals a specific time period, establishes a chronological order, and focuses upon the immediacy of the events to follow.

A convention of all the provincial leaders meeting in Shushan with King Ahasuerus, a refusal to obey the king's command, the authorization and selection of Esther for queen, and the resolution of a short-lived conspiracy against the king have already transpired. Chapter 3 focuses on Haman the Agagite. We see his promotion to a new position, his ancestry, his accomplishments, and his failure.

Origins and Attributes

Who is Haman and what is an Agagite? An Agagite was a person of the lineage of Agag, a king of the Amalekites. Who are the Amalekites? They are the descendants of Amalek. Finally, who was Amalek? Genesis 36:12 states, "And Timna was concubine to Eliphaz Esau's son; and she bare to Eliphaz, Amalek...." Amalek's grandfather, Esau, the twin brother of Jacob, had no interest in God or spiritual and eternal things. He lived for the here and now, for self-gratification and personal exaltation. This was Haman's ancestry, and he followed in those evil ways, having the same interests as Esau. The New Testament refers to these interests as the "works of the flesh" (see Gal. 5:19-21) and teaches that these works are self-destructive and must be dealt with severely. They must be crucified in order to be purged out of existence.

This truth is not new. It is taught in the Old Testament in First Samuel chapter 15. Samuel, God's spokesman, went to King Saul with a message, a directive to annihilate the Amalekites. This was the same Amalek who was later identified as Haman's ancestor. The reason for this harsh instruction was because of the ill treatment Amalek had directed toward God's people, Israel, on their way from Egypt to the Promised Land.

Saul was commanded to administer God's orders. First Samuel 15:9 reveals that Saul did not fully carry out these commands. He took the job of determining what was good and bad into his own hands. He made his own decision, which was different from God's command. Saul spared the king of the Amalekites, along with the best of the spoil. The result was that Israel was condemned to battle the Amalekites from generation to generation. Saul's failure to carry out God's orders surfaced later in Israel's history in the actions of Haman (an Agagite).

The segments of Saul's story assume additional significance as an allegory of the world today. Saul, representing mankind, has an enemy, Amalek. Amalek is man's sinful nature. Mankind is not dealing with its enemy as

God's Word has instructed. This explains why the world is the way it is. In addition, the story demonstrates where such self-destructive behavior leads.

This brief background of Haman outlines the history behind the life style he had inherited. Everything he did was allowed, but his actions were not condoned or blessed. Allowed but not blessed, this Haman was a leader whose actions came out of and were produced by his inherited nature stemming from his background. (This is a good picture of man—his nature and actions—who also inherited his weakness.)

Esther 3:1-2

The drama continues. Haman is promoted by King Ahasuerus to the position of prime minister. This is truly a lofty position as Esther 3:1-2 attests: "...and [the king] advanced him, and set his seat above all the princes...And all the king's servants, that were in the king's gate, bowed, and reverenced Haman...."

Promotion, Prestige, and Pride

This promotion brought accolades and honors. Verse 2 reveals that all bowed or were in submission to this leader, "for the king had so commanded." The Hebrew word for *commanded* here means "to constitute." From this same root comes *constitution,* which means "a set of laws establishing that which is legal." God made man in His image and likeness. One of God's, and therefore man's, attributes is freedom of choice. God has also given man His Word, which is His law. God's desire has always been that man would choose to obey His law, but if man did not choose Him, then he would submit to some other. It is in this light that we see how Haman had position, power, and people in submission to himself. Haman's role also provides perspective and understanding of the character and behavior of one who exalts himself.

Haman's promotion happened very shortly after Mordecai's intervention which had saved King Ahasuerus' life. The word translated "after" in the first verse comes from the Hebrew root word *achar*, meaning, "coming from behind"; the original Hebrew implies "losing no time in doing so."

The rapid development of the drama verifies the sense of "coming from behind speedily" as part of Haman's persona. One meaning of Haman's name is "splendid." Another Hebrew word sounds similar to Haman and means "commotion or disturbance." Hebrew literature plays on words to create irony. In the translation of Haman's name this irony emerges. Haman appears to be splendid, but is in reality the direct cause of chaos.

This translation of Haman's name parallels the description given in Second Corinthians 11:14: "And no marvel; for satan himself is transformed into an angel of light." The character Haman portrays evil masquerading as light or goodness, and his role in this drama is that of antichrist—the embodiment of the spirit of evil. The charmer turns out to be mankind's destroyer.

Ultimately, satan is the epitome of all that Haman represents in the drama. Satan's stance is anti-God, anti-Christ, anti-Semitic, and anti-Christian. His charming and deceptive ideologies and doctrines manifest themselves through his evil operations This affects mankind through both religious and political realms. His final mode of operation will culminate in a human form, an incarnation (if it can be called that).

Just as the character and nature of the Spirit of God became incarnate through His Son, Jesus Christ, satan will be doing his own impersonation through a man who will be accepted as the Messiah by deceived Jews and Gentiles. However, the end result will be a counterfeit person with a nature identical to satan's. He is the master impersonator and deceiver. He, by his nature, is pride personified.

As we look upon all the peoples of the earth and the various political and religious ideologies holding sway over mankind, we are witnessing the rise and promotion of this Hamanic spirit. (There were other princes in Ahasuerus's kingdom, but it was Haman who received the promotion.) Man's history records numerous types of political and religious systems, but now a system is being promoted to incorporate both spheres.

As a political ideology, the system is called the "new world order." As a religious ideology, it is represented by the New Age Movement, which is a religious extension of humanism. This religious system, which is rapidly growing, promotes the glorification of man or the human spirit and even nature itself. We know this spiritual philosophy is evil because it opposes the first commandment given to Moses. Deuteronomy 6:5 commands, "And thou shalt love the Lord thy God with all thine heart and with all thy soul and with all thy might." Jesus repeated this in Matthew 22:37-38: "…Thou shalt love the Lord thy God with all thy heart, and with all thy soul, and with all thy mind. This is the first and great commandment."

This planet and its people could be divided into segments in which religious ideologies hold controlling positions. We could label them Christian, Judaic, Islamic, (for the monotheistic ones), and add Hindu and other major and minor religions which rule over the inhabitants of earth. The New Age philosophy is spreading rapidly by the spirit of humanism. It is moving to incorporate and unite all into a common religion based on human logic and rationale. New Age epitomizes the glorification of the accomplishments of the spirit of man.

Haman's seat was promoted above all other princes. Likewise, humanism's position of power has been elevated over the whole earth and is very prominent indeed. The preaching of humanism and the exaltation of human potential and power is encompassing the world at all levels and from all directions—from pulpit to podium. It is including religious, governmental, educational, economic, and all other spheres of influence that hold mankind subject. Submission to and reverence toward humanism is multiplying, for preaching of humanism is sweeping the globe. Its laws and precepts are established by human rationale and logic, advocating these as the sole source of truth and calling for acceptance of these alone.

Multitudes are now choosing deism over theism. Most people have a spiritual awareness of God, but many adopt "dress codes" of their own choosing. The God of Scripture has clearly defined what His dress code is.

We can see a parallel between the sudden elevation of Haman over all of the princes and that of present-day humanism as it rapidly absorbs the allegiance of multitudes of people through its religious and political advocates. As Haman received reverence, so New Age humanism is rapidly receiving reverence and acceptance.

Who is this Mordecai? In the preceding chapters he played the role of guardian to Esther and performed flawlessly. Esther 2:20 records, "Esther had not yet shewed her kindred nor her people; as Mordecai had charged her: for Esther did the commandment of Mordecai, like as when she was brought up by him." The name Mordecai, or Marduke as it is sometimes translated, means "a deity of Mars." We are only considering the "deity" part of this meaning as we continue this symbolism of Mordecai as he portrays the Living Word.

The Savior in Scripture is introduced in the Gospel of John as deity personified; the habitation of the Living Word was with and literally was God. "In the beginning was the Word, and the Word was with God, and the Word was God" (Jn. 1:1). Scripture says He was the only begotten and first-born of the Father. This heaven-orchestrated birth gave Him both a physical and a spiritual identity here on earth. As a physical being, He now had a relationship with man, but His relationship with His heavenly Father gave Him His spiritual identity. The Living Word truly is deity personified, and His earthly name is Jesus (*Yeshua* in Hebrew)!

This Jesus was given the guardianship of the Church and now stands as the sole antagonist of satan. He is an obstacle to satan and his strategies for achieving his personal desires, just as Mordecai was Haman's sole antagonist and obstacle.

Similarly, as Haman received reverence, so also New Age humanism, through what it advocates, is giving reverence to satan or the god of this world. New Age will sweep all people of all religions into its fold except for those who are faithful to the Living Word and belong to the Father of

Might. These include all born-again and faithful Christians as well as the Jewish remnant faithfully waiting for their promised Messiah. The Word of the biblical God, the Living Word, is not just in book form. It is planted in the hearts of the faithful believers by His Eternal Spirit! These believers will not give reverence to this Hamanic humanistic spirit and its ideology.

All were subservient to Haman except Mordecai. This is the setting where these two characters first meet in the Book of Esther. Mordecai was initially portrayed in his guardianship to Esther as the Church is related to Jesus the Living Word. Now he is shown in his antagonistic relationship to Haman who represents the antichrist spirit.

The god of this world, satan, is the source of the antichrist spirit, as well as the prophesied antichrist himself. This will be a man who will be totally deceived and dominated by satan. A person might think that this man will be hideous or grotesque, but according to Scripture, he will be a charmer, one adept at using flatteries, and an impersonator of truth. As in the Garden of Eden, he will continuously epitomize pride, he will believe his own ideas and rationale to be truth, and he will deceive others into believing them also. The ultimate deception is recorded in Revelation 6:2: "And I saw, and behold a white horse: and he that sat on him had a bow; and a crown was given unto him: and he went forth conquering, and to conquer."

White horses were first used by the Roman generals when they led processions celebrating their victories in battle and the peace which ensued. So the white horse of Revelation 6:2 reflects an achievement or victory, the establishment of peace, with prosperity following in its footsteps. The rider on this white horse carries a harmless bow, without arrows, signifying an absence of conventional weapons. Nevertheless, this rider is given a crown, symbolizing authority and power. So without conventional weapons, but with a crown, this rider will go forth, signifying that he has conquered and achieved world dominion.

To the world it will appear that the Prince of Truth has finally arrived and that the world has finally reached its "utopia." However, Revelation 6 continues with the following horsemen: the second one is on a red horse symbolizing war; the third one, on a black horse symbolizing famine and pestilence; and the horse of the last rider is a pale horse symbolizing death and Hades.

Reflecting on the preceding scenario, the lead horseman, despite the appearance of splendor, will actually be the lead horseman of this destructive array of horsemen. The horseman on the lead white horse is nothing more than the *glorified deceiver*. In reality, this horseman will be the instrument responsible for unleashing horrendous wars, followed by famine and pestilence, which will lead to incomprehensible numbers of dead.

The Hamanic or New Age spirit appears to be so splendid, but in reality will be the leader of the horror described fully throughout the Book of Revelation—a time of tribulation. The words of Jesus in Matthew 24:21–22 are very descriptive of this time period: "For then shall be great tribulation, such as was not since the beginning of the world to this time, no, nor ever shall be. And except those days should be shortened, there should no flesh be saved: but for the elect's sake those days shall be shortened."

The lead horseman will be nothing more than an impersonation of the true Messiah, without the power or the ability to bring in an everlasting utopia. Truth doesn't tolerate, neither can it be duplicated by impersonations. God is Truth and He is totally sufficient.

> *How art thou fallen from heaven, O Lucifer, son of the morning! how art thou cut down to the ground, which didst weaken the nations! For thou has said in thine heart, I will ascend into heaven, I will exalt my throne above the stars of God: I will sit also upon the mount of the congregation, in the sides of the north: I will ascend above the heights of the clouds; I will be like the most High. Yet thou shalt be brought down to hell, to the sides of the pit* (Isaiah 14:12-15).

Esther, chapters 3–10, gives further evidence to substantiate the picture in Isaiah 14:12-15, revealing how satan arrived on earth, his intentions, his works, and his ultimate destiny.

Eternal Relations

In contrast to the rebellious relationship of satan against the Almighty (who created him and appointed him to a position of power and glory), is the relationship of a loving God who reaches out to man. When He establishes such a bond, He calls these people His friends. Scripture is filled with examples of God's interaction with individuals.

In James 2:23 the writer records, "And the scripture was fulfilled which saith, Abraham believed God, and it was imputed unto him for righteousness: and he was called the Friend of God." A further reference, Exodus 33:11, states, "And the Lord spake unto Moses face to face, as a man speaketh unto his friend. And he turned again into the camp:

but his servant Joshua, the son of Nun, a young man, departed not out of the tabernacle." Yet another reference, Second Chronicles 20:7, records, "Art not Thou our God, who didst drive out the inhabitants of this land before Thy people Israel, and gavest it to the seed of Abraham Thy friend for ever?" A final reference, John 15:15, declares, "Henceforth I call you not servants; for the servant knoweth not what his lord doeth: but I have called you friends; for all things that I have heard of My Father I have made known unto you."

These four Scriptures reveal four truths.

1. God identifies with people as friends.

2. God will not hide anything that He sees as beneficial.

3. There are things God has promised to do.

4. God wants us to be involved with Him.

The criteria for enjoying friendship with God is revealed in John 1:12: "But as many as received Him [Jesus], to them gave He [the Holy Spirit] power to become the sons of God [the Father], even to them that believe on His name [Jesus]."

Obeying this command allows you to receive what Jesus has personally done for you: forgiveness of your sin because of His death on the cross, a new life because of the work of the Holy Spirit of God, and then acceptance as God's son/daughter, even as Jesus who was called "the only begotten son of God" in John 3:16. Added to this is the truth of John 15:15, a statement filled with promise: "Henceforth I call you not servants; for the servant knoweth not what his lord doeth: but I have called you friends; for all things that I have heard of My Father I have made known unto you." Jesus constantly made reference to His Father in Heaven.

Why is so much time and space dedicated to the topic of friendship with God? The truths revealed in the Book of Esther could very well be obscure and meaningless unless you are God's friend. If you are not, you need to know how to establish this friendship.

First, Scripture states the obvious in Romans 3:23: "For all have sinned, and come short of the glory of God." Hebrews 9:22 continues, "...without shedding of blood is no remission."

Further, Scripture emphasizes that the sacrifice had to be a lamb without blemish. Jesus Christ was the unblemished Lamb. He offered Himself freely as the supreme, final, and effective sacrifice. All we, as sinners, have to do is to acknowledge our guilt through a prayer of confession, and God will give us the eternal life He promised. When we do this, our relationship begins.

If you have never done this before, would you pause for a moment and accept God's great gift? Do it now. If you have taken the time and sincerely followed these scriptural instructions, you will experience new realities, particularly in the following two areas: First, the question of, "God, who are you?" (the question that all human beings are born with), will no longer exist. Second, thoughts about dying and eternity will no longer be filled with uncertainty. You will know because your spirit and God's Spirit have entered into an eternal relationship. For some, the awareness may be instantaneous, while for others, the assurance of this reality will reveal itself progressively.

What may appear to be a digression from the drama of Esther is not a digression at all. We see and hear, as the Scripture declares, with spiritual eyes and ears. People who do not have spiritual life certainly do not have spiritual sight and hearing. We hope that many have made a decision to enter into friendship with God at this point. Now, we will continue to venture into the truths of the Book of Esther with enlightened eyes which see God's truth.

A Decision of Faith

Referring back to Isaiah 14:12-15, five times the speaker, satan, repeats the phrase, "I will." Each "I will" represents a selfish diabolical goal. "I will": (a) ascend into Heaven; (b) exalt my throne; (c) sit upon the mount of the congregation; (d) ascend above the clouds; and (e) be like the most high God. All of these reflect the personal desires of Haman! How does he go about achieving his goals of having absolute control and becoming a figure of worship?

Esther 3:2-4

In Esther 3:2 it seems as if Haman almost attains what he wants. Only Mordecai (Jesus the Living Word) refuses to bow to Haman! Mordecai reveals the reason for his unwillingness to submit or subject himself to Haman. First he explains himself to the king's servants and then to Haman. He tells them "that he is a Jew."

This term "Jew" should be the key reason for any person not to bow down to the Hamanic spirit of this day. The Hamanic spirit is a spirit synonymous with satan, antichrist, the spirit of this world, the flesh, and everything else that exalts itself above the knowledge of God. Jesus contended with the Jews of His day who gloried in their bloodline. They thought this was sufficient identification as a Jew.

Jesus, however, made it clear that a Jew was one like Abraham, one who believed and responded with an act of obedience when God spoke to him.

In Matthew 4:1–11 we find the story of the temptations of Jesus in the wilderness. This took place immediately after His baptism in the Jordan. At His baptism He received God's seal of approval. An audible voice from Heaven was heard saying, "This is My beloved Son in whom I am well pleased" (Mt. 3:17b).

This sign, the elevated position of Jesus, finds its parallel in Esther 2:19: "And when the virgins were gathered together the second time, then Mordecai sat in the king's gate." This certainly symbolizes a position of power within the structure of the king's kingdom, one undoubtedly received because Esther had been chosen as queen.

Esther 3:5

A bold and authoritative Mordecai appears. Mordecai will not kneel down or pay Haman honor. This infuriates Haman!

Similarly, Jesus refused to submit to satan and to succumb to the temptations offered to Him in the wilderness. His refusal infuriated the ruler of this world. His answer was identical to Mordecai's, "I am a Jew." Jesus' words were, "…Get thee behind Me [or 'get lost'] Satan: for it is written, Thou shalt worship the Lord thy God and Him only shalt thou serve" (Lk. 4:8). Jesus was saying, "I am a Jew." He was making reference to the first, and most important, of the Ten Commandments God had given to Moses. These commandments gave Israel their special identification. It was their God and His code of laws that separated them from other people. Everyone who accepted this God, believed, and applied these laws were called Jews. This alone is the determining factor as to who is a true Jew, a faithful Jew, and a believing Jew. It is an action that outwardly reveals one's faith.

Haman's Plot: Vengeance Engineered

Esther 3:5-11

Haman is infuriated. "And he thought scorn to lay hands on Mordecai alone; for they had shown him the people of Mordecai: wherefore Haman sought to destroy all the Jews that were throughout the whole kingdom of Ahasuerus, even the people of Mordecai" (Esther 3:6).

Haman petitions the king with accusations against them and intends to accomplish his goals. There are half-truths in Haman's accusation: "...their laws are diverse from all people, neither keep they the king's laws: therefore, it is not for the king's profit to suffer them" (Esther 3:7). The king accepts Haman's report and grants his request.

Likewise, we see the "ruler of this world" working with one purpose in mind...the annihilation of God's chosen people and all truly born-again believers. This is to satisfy the evil desires of his heart. We see the inequity of this situation vividly in our world today. The question is, "How can a loving, holy God allow what is happening on this earth of His? Is He all-knowing or not?" The trial of Job depicts a similar dilemma. In this encounter, satan comes before the throne of God with accusations that Job worships God only because He has abundantly blessed him. With this twisted statement (which God knew was a lie), satan was permitted to test Job. In doing this, God unmasked the lie of satan to the liar himself. From satan's perspective, what he had said was truth. This was simply because the principle he rules by has been to buy the allegiance and loyalty of men through the avenues of their weaknesses and their carnal desires.

However, the real truth is that people who correctly worship the true God do so because they have experienced divine love. Do you worship God because you have experienced this divine love, or do you have a form of worship based upon selected scriptural texts or isolated doctrinal teachings? Are you following instructions and traditions that are appealing to your personal taste, but only produce a "pseudo" sense of security?

After Haman presents his case, he asks for permission to destroy the Jewish people and the request is granted. The parallel of this edict in human history is manifested through anti-Semitism against God's people, Israel. Today, it is obvious that much money is spent to accomplish the destruction of Israel. Because this evil is in operation, does this mean that the King of the Universe does not know what is going on? God forbid! He spoke this world into existence! It continues to exist because "He upholds it by the word of His power" (Heb. 1:3). Further, Scripture states that heaven and earth may pass away, but the Word of the Lord abides forever (see Lk. 21:33). God loves His chosen people, and He has promised to deliver them. He cannot lie. Their deliverance is assured!

Esther 3:12–15

What appears in verse 15 to be a mutually satisfying decision holds prophetic significance.

...And the king and Haman sat down to drink, but the city of Shushan was perplexed.

Remember, the king portrays God, and Haman symbolizes the god of this world, satan. We now see the very essence of good and of evil embarking upon a collision course. It is as though both are at ease, but what has been set in motion cannot be altered.

The Living Bible translates the latter half of verse 15 this way: "As the city fell into confusion and panic." Confusion and panic are mild words to describe what lies ahead for Israel, Jerusalem, and the whole world. Is the same loving God who allowed Job to go through his horrible trials still in control of this mess? When the false, masquerading Christ (Haman) achieves his goal of power and control, he will demand the reverence and worship which belongs only to God. At that point confusion and panic will set in for Jews who refuse to bow to him. God has left some clear instructions for these Jews during that time. He gave them through His Son Jesus. They are recorded in Matthew 24:14-31. Read on—there is hope!

Chapter 4

When Reality Sets In

Esther and the Church's Qualifications

Esther 4:1–9

Alert to the danger engineered by Haman, Mordecai realizes that nothing short of direct intervention by the king will save the Jews from annihilation. Sitting in sackcloth and ashes, Mordecai created a scene which prompted Esther to send Hatach to investigate. Mordecai now engages chamberlain Hatach who now serves as the messenger between Esther and himself.

Esther's vital role in the drama takes on a "do or die" attitude. "...He [Mordecai)] gave him [Hatach] the copy of the writing of the decree that was given at Shushan to destroy them [Jews], to *shew* it unto Esther, and to *declare* it unto her, and to *charge* her that she should go unto the king, to make supplication unto him, and to make request before him for her people" (Esther 4:8). Esther has always been faithful to Mordecai. Will she fail him in this situation? Esther becomes disturbed, anxious, and inquisitive about the situation taking place. She immediately sends Hatach to Mordecai for advice and direction. Hatach returns to Esther with a reply from Mordecai. Not only was she *told*, but she was also *shown* a copy of the royal decree that authorizes the killing of the Jews. Thus, a double witness establishes the truth of the message.

Isolated and preoccupied, Esther was quite ignorant of the severity of the situation that existed. The message from Mordecai (the Living Word) comes by the messenger Hatach (Holy Spirit) to show (see) and declare (hear) the problem and to give her instructions and guidance as well. These instructions *charged her* and commanded her to go to the king and make supplication, requesting his immediate intervention.

Just as Mordecai was alert to the danger, Jesus the Living Word is fully aware of all that transpires. He has the ability to get the attention of His Church, just as Mordecai got Esther's attention. The Holy Spirit, the promise of the Father given to the Son, is active in this relationship. Likewise, Hatach, here representing the Holy Spirit as the communicator, serves to carry messages between Mordecai and Esther.

Esther became disturbed. So too, when the peace of God lifts from a true believer, the believer becomes disturbed. After personally experiencing the peace that passes all understanding, the believer's spirit immediately is alerted when this peace leaves. For restoration to take place, the next logical step is to inquire and seek counsel. The child of God will turn to the Living Word to seek the "what and why." God is sovereign and faithful. Therefore, He will give clear directions and will reveal the next correct step. If these steps are obediently followed, the "what's and the why's" will be exposed as the actions are taken. We are to rest in Him with the knowledge that He does supply. Hatach was Esther's avenue of communication. The Holy Spirit is the avenue of communication for the true believer. When a believer inquires honestly, exercising faith in God, he can always count on a truthful response from his Master.

Mordecai commissioned Hatach "to show and tell" Esther the edict. She received a double witness confirming the message. Individuals who hear truth become liable for the course of their actions. Since God has given free will, they can either accept or reject this truth. Acceptance of revealed truth brings promised earthly and eternal blessing. Rejection of the truth will usher in its tragic consequences.

Truth Directs the Choice

Esther 4:10-15

Esther's response should be immediate and positive, alert to how her position uniquely qualifies her to intercede for her people, the Jewish race. However, Esther balks and hesitates, for this message brings a challenge to the comfort to which she has become accustomed. Esther states, "All the...people...do know, that whosoever...shall come unto the king into the inner court, who is not called, there is one law of his to put him to death...but I have not been called" (Esther 4:11).

No one is in a better position to help. No one! Mordecai's call raises two issues for Esther. First, is she forgetting her heritage? She is a Jewess. Does she think she will escape when all the other Jews are killed? God will use another source to save His people, but she will be doomed unless she *acts*. "For if thou altogether holdest thy peace at this time, then shall there enlargement and deliverance arise to the Jews from another place; but thou and thy father's house shall be destroyed..." (Esther 4:14).

The second challenge Mordecai raises is that perhaps, just perhaps, Esther is at the right place at the right time in God's plan: "and who knoweth whether thou art come to the kingdom for such a time as this" (Esther 4:14b).

A fascinating parallel can be drawn from Scripture. The Word of God specifically declares that the Lord Jesus is coming back. It clearly defines events, conditions, mental attitudes, and life styles of earth's inhabitants just prior to the Lord's return. It also delineates many other prophetic signs (which are currently being fulfilled) that will usher in the Messiah. We have been told the signs of His coming. We have a copy of God's Word, the Bible, sent forth from His headquarters in *Israel* and we are charged with the following: "Make yourself ready to go in before the King." The admonition is simple, yet powerful: listen, obey, watch, and work. Scripture warns people not to be caught off guard. Christ will return as a thief in the night, and we are not to become attached to this world, regardless of the pleasures and cares that so easily become our preoccupations.

The dialogue between Esther and Mordecai is analogous to how people, even believers, dialogue with God. How many times do we renege, or pull back from the commands of God because something of ours (so we think) is being jeopardized by what we have been asked to do? Will it affect my health or my wealth or interfere with my personal plans? These seem to be the prominent concerns. Further, aren't we in a similar and desperate dilemma today? The antichrist spirit, and eventually the antichrist himself, are the perpetrators of an edict, a death warrant, for all those who have a relationship with the Living Word, Jesus.

Mordecai informs Esther that if she holds back, deliverance will come from another source; however, the converse is that if she is obedient, she may become the channel for deliverance. What certainty undergirds the Word of God! When God speaks to His people, His pronouncements are reliable. What a wonderful way to live, especially when all other voices contain the quivering weakness of uncertainty.

Wisdom Makes the Choice

Esther 4:15-17

Returning to the drama unfolding in the Book of Esther, Mordecai graphically states the desperate situation. Esther finally grasps the gravity of the hour and begins to act. She stops rationalizing and starts moving. Esther is absolutely convinced. She makes her decision and confirms this by going into action.

Just as Esther responded to the challenge presented her, so too, many believers are turning their attention to the prophetic Word. These Scriptures are becoming vivid through present day events which are taking place rapidly. These believers have not only made their decisions for Christ, but they are acting upon them. We not only see this in local churches, but we hear of mass ingatherings worldwide as God continues to open doors. A spiritual renewal is taking place in the Iron Curtain countries, along with many other countries around the globe.

However, we also see many believers in Western society who are "dozing at the wheel," so to speak. It is our duty to take action as Esther did. We pray that God will use us to see the ones in jeopardy. May we blow our horns or sound an alarm, awakening those who have fallen into slumber. Today the Church has a prophetic blueprint of God's Word in its possession. This contains many prophecies related to end times. She has historical evidences up to this day that confirm many prophecies. Surely these should convince and motivate the Church. These evidences testify to the validity of the Living Word, even as Esther was motivated by those things that were declared unto her.

Chapter 5

The Throne of Grace

With the help of Hatach, chapter 4 of Esther closes on a positive note. Mordecai and Esther are united in a common cause: to save those of Jewish heritage (including Esther). The events of chapters 1 through 4 cover a span of approximately 12 years. In chapter 5 the drama of Esther accelerates.

Esther 5:1

Esther sees the gravity of the situation. Time is very precious. The Scripture account reads, "Now it came to pass on the third day, that Esther put on her royal apparel, and stood in the inner court of the king's house, over against the king's house..." (Esther 5:1).

The inner court is a large area in front of the throne room where the king sits. He can see out but others cannot see in. However, the glory that radiates is enough to confirm his presence. Esther does not take a position on the outer fringes of the inner court. Rather, she makes absolutely sure that the king will not miss seeing her. She is not going to be overlooked.

What an interesting parallel this is to the Bride of Christ, the Church. In First Corinthians 15:51–53 we read:

Behold, I show you a mystery; we shall not all sleep, but we shall all be changed, in a moment, in the twinkling of an eye, at the last trump, for the trumpet shall sound and the dead shall be raised incorruptible, and we shall be changed. For this corruptible must put on incorruption and the mortal must put on immortality (1 Corinthians 15:51-53).

Acceptable Requirements

Esther 5:1

Esther puts on her royal attire. She has been fasting for a three-day period. (See Esther 4:16.)

The writer is referring to a literal abstention from eating—fasting. But could this imply something greater? The meaning of the Hebrew word for fasting is "to cover the mouth." In Esther's case the meaning is quite clear: "to stop eating."

The mouth is also used for speaking. How often mankind abuses the power of speech. Perhaps a further observation concerning Esther's "covering of the mouth" could be that when she ceased talking and looking for excuses as to why she could not obey, she was able to see the gravity of the situation clearly. She decided to listen.

Perhaps today's Church is too busy "talking." Perhaps she, too, should stop talking, use her spiritual eyes and ears, and receive a clear understanding of what her Mordecai is saying. In Isaiah 6:1–7 Isaiah exhorts the reader concerning the importance of clean lips:

In the year that king Uzziah died I saw also the Lord sitting upon a throne, high and lifted up, and His train filled the temple. Above it stood the seraphims:

each one had six wings; with twain he covered his face, and with twain he covered his feet, and with twain he did fly. And one cried unto another, and said, holy, holy, holy, is the Lord of hosts: the whole earth is full of His glory. And the posts of the door moved at the voice of him that cried, and the house was filled with smoke. Then said I, Woe is me, for I am undone; because I am a man of unclean lips, and I dwell in the midst of a people of unclean lips: for mine eyes have seen the King, the Lord of hosts. Then flew one of the seraphims unto me, having a live coal in his hand, which he had taken with the tongs from off the altar: and he laid it upon my mouth, and said, Lo, this hath touched thy lips; and thine iniquity is taken away, and thy sin purged (Isaiah 6:1-7).

This passage describes the difference between man and God. God is holy. The same "lips" that spoke life into existence speak in divine judgment, requiring the forfeiture of life. Two passages that describe the anger of God in judgment include: "For the Lord thy God is a consuming fire, even a jealous God" (Deut. 4:24), and "For our God is a consuming fire" (Heb. 12:29).

Man, according to Scripture, has a fallen or sinful nature, one that is weak and cannot in itself live up to the standards of a holy God. This nature has been condemned to death by a holy and just God. So the basic difference between the biblical God and man is their characters, natures, and wills. There is a definite collision course unless someone comes to the rescue

All things that are not of God and that challenge His will and His authority will be destroyed. The passage cited earlier,

First Corinthians 15:15–53, describes the new royal robe that the redeemed (the Church) will be given. Esther, a symbol of the Church, knew what would make the king angry. She also knew the penalty for this. However, she knew the king could be influenced by beauty. Beauty would bring joy and pleasure to him.

The Word of God reveals there are things that please Him and things that displease Him, some even to the point of anger. Faith and obedience are His good pleasure, but rebellion fires His holy anger.

What if Esther had put on a few pounds, obscuring the defined features of her beauty? It will be wise for the Church to examine herself. Are there extra pounds because of overindulgence in the things of this world? Has the Church become overly active, duped into believing that a performance of commonly accepted rituals and duties can purchase God's approval?

Esther understood and applied the truth of Hebrews 12:28: "Wherefore we receiving a kingdom which cannot be moved, let us have grace, whereby we may serve God acceptably with reverence and godly fear." This preparation should be the concern of each individual—the imminent donning of royal robes.

John 1:17 notes, "For the law was given by Moses, but grace and truth came by Jesus Christ." Jesus is God's incarnate display of all His goodness and truth. Those who plan to enter the inner court of the King of Glory and enjoy a favorable reception, must prepare themselves properly to come into His presence. One receives grace and truth by accepting the Living Word. All other preparations are challenges to what He has declared to be acceptable and are nothing more than rebellious fantasies.

Her Grand Entrance and Reception

Esther 5:2

Esther finds favor with her king. What a truly glorious and dramatic moment this is! The account records, "...when the king saw Esther the queen standing in the court, that she obtained favour in his sight: and the king held out to Esther the golden sceptre.... So Esther drew near, and touched the top of the sceptre" (Esther 5:2).

The scepter in this verse has many different meanings in the original Hebrew text: "a scion, a rod, a staff." Each had various uses. Two of these uses were the king's issuing a command for debate and his signaling the execution of a royal order—a ruling of "so be it." This scepter symbolized the power emanating from his throne.

It is interesting and very revealing that Esther was in the inner court for only moments when she was made welcome. In essence, she was invited to share the power and authority that only the king could wield. Further, no one, *absolutely no one* except the king, was permitted to touch this scepter. The Hebrew word translated "touched" also carries the definitions of "draw near (nigh), join, and acquire." There is the sense of an intimate union in this word. The king is saying, "What is mine is yours." He wanted Esther to know that all of his resources were hers.

So, too, will the true Church, born of God's grace, living by God's grace, and trusting God's grace, be favorably received by the King of the Universe. When the Church meets Jesus Christ, the Living Word, in the clouds, she will be clothed with royal robes. She will enter into the inner court to be received before the heavenly throne of majesty and power. The offer to share the power and possessions of her heavenly King will also be extended.

Esther entered the inner court on the third day. Why the third day? What transpired on days one and two? Did Esther and Mordecai unite for one specific purpose during these two days of preparation? Were days one and two incorporated into the three-day period that culminated in Esther's entrance? I believe on the third day when she made her entrance, she was also fasting, in absolute readiness, having done all that she could do to prepare for this unscheduled appearance before the king. Mordecai's message had abruptly dislodged her false sense of security and comfort. Because of her isolation, she had been ignorant of the death edict that had been ordered.

In this aspect also, Esther parallels today's Church. The quickening pace of fulfilled prophecy sounds an alarm. Just as Esther needed the king's intervention to stop the evil that had been set in motion by Haman, and she prepared herself for her first uninvited appearance before him, similarly, the Church has been in the process of preparing herself for an unprecedented appearance, a uniting with the Living Word at the sound of the trumpet. The Church, too, will be coming before the eternal Sovereign with a message about the evil that has been unleashed in a segment of His Kingdom, the earth.

What do the two days of fasting and prayer by Esther and Mordecai represent? I believe they are symbolic of the 2,000-year period that began with the call of Abraham to be the father of God's chosen people (Israel) and continued through the ministry of Israel's last prophet, Malachi. The two days could also symbolize the 2,000-year period in which the Church has been in the process of formation. In both applications, the God of Truth unveils the truth concerning man, this planet, and satan. Satan is bent on one purpose—to utterly destroy God's creation and all of mankind by subverting God's laws. Both applications find support in Scripture.

One reference, Second Peter 3:8, says, "But, beloved, be not ignorant of this one thing, that one day is with the Lord as a thousand years, and a thousand years as one day." Another, Hosea 6:1–2, states, "Come, and let us return unto the Lord: for He hath torn, and He will heal us; He hath smitten, and He will bind us up. After two days will He revive us; in the third day He will raise us up, and we shall live in His sight."

Do Scriptures also depict the 2,000-years of Israel's history from the point of God's scattering of His chosen people, Israel, into all nations? If so, then He promises restitution and declares that they will live in His sight.

What about the Church, those who were born by a mighty act of God's power on the Day of Pentecost? Her population has been continually increasing by God's divine power and might, through the working of His Holy Spirit. Can we find evidence in Scripture that imbues this historical occurrence with symbolic significance? I believe the events recorded in the two banquets given by Esther provide the necessary connection.

Petition Granted: A People Saved

Esther 5:3

The king knows that something is bothering Esther. She approaches him; he hadn't called her. Nevertheless, she pleases him and he wants to please her. He makes it quite clear that he will give her what she desires and the extent to which he will go to satisfy her request. "...It shall be even given thee to the half of the kingdom. And Esther answered, If it seem good unto the king, let the king and Haman come this day unto the banquet that I have prepared for him" (Esther 5:3-4). Haman is summoned immediately, and they come to the banquet that Esther has prepared. Again, at the banquet, the king makes it quite clear that he is here to grant Esther her every request. All she needs to do is ask. Esther's response almost seems coy as she does not reveal her specific request but rather invites the king and Haman to a second banquet. Not until then will she make her petition known.

Approximately 2,000 years have passed since the inception of the Church on the Day of Pentecost. Mordecai was given a seat of power; likewise, the Son of God. Hebrews 1:8 says, "But unto the Son He saith, Thy throne, O God, is for ever and ever: a sceptre of righteousness is the sceptre of Thy kingdom." Just as Esther was given the right to go before the throne of the king when called, so the Church has been given authority to enter the throne room of the Almighty. Hebrews 4:16 states, "Let us therefore come boldly unto the throne of grace, that we may obtain mercy, and find grace to help in time of need."

Hebrews 8:1 continues, "Now of the things which we have spoken this is the sum: We have such an high priest, who is set on the right hand of the throne of the Majesty in the heavens." Is this seat at the right hand of the Majesty the throne coveted by lucifer? Does satan become infuriated each time he appears before God? In the Book of Job the writer reports that satan appeared before the throne and God required an accounting of where he had been and what he had been doing. Is satan infuriated with the Living Word now seated there? Is his preoccupation with destroying God's people an attempt to annul the Living Word's seat of authority as High Priest?

Consider: if no one comes to the Living Word as High Priest, the office is meaningless, the position vacuous. Yes, this is satan's ultimate purpose—the total annihilation of God's people. His tactics incorporate deception and the adulteration of truth, making the liberating power of truth null and void, whether by using the subtlety of polluting the truth or by the direct assault of premeditated genocide.

For 2,000 years, or two banquet days, the Church, symbolized by Esther, has been coming into the presence of the heavenly Sovereign. The contents of her prayers and petitions have reflected, even as Esther's countenance, that there are major concerns. Surely this has caught the attention of the King.

Satan has also been coming, still glorying in the fact that he, too, can present himself there. Each time he leaves, though, he must look at the Living Word who no longer simply refuses to bow, but now refuses to even stand up. This gesture speaks volumes. It says, "I will not give you even the least bit of recognition, no matter what powers you are capable of exhibiting!"

Happiness Without Contentment

Esther 5:11-14

Haman is pleased with all that his maneuvering has accomplished. On one hand he is ecstatic. In Esther 5:11 he boasts to his wife of his promotion: "And Haman told them of the glory of his riches...and all the things wherein the king had promoted him, and how he had advanced him above the princes and servants of the king." The

Living Bible phrases the latter segment in this way: "…and how he had become the greatest man in the kingdom next to the king himself"(Esther 5:11 TLB).

On the other hand Haman is still not satisfied! He wants to be equated with the total power of the king. He also wants everyone to bow to and revere him. He leaves the presence of the king, having attended this banquet at the order of the king. He does not return home content, however. Mordecai is the stumbling block that stands in the way of Haman. All the wealth in the world will not be enough because greed and an insatiable thirst for power still blind him. Esther 5:13 says, "Yet all this availeth me nothing, so long as I see Mordecai the Jew sitting at the king's gate."

Incredibly, Haman's delight in being summoned to the banquet by the king is stifled by Mordecai's presence as he passes him by. Esther 5:9 says, "…but when Haman saw Mordecai in the king's gate, that he stood not up, nor moved for him, he was full of indignation against Mordecai." Consequently, Haman avidly embraces the advice of his wife, Zeresh, and his fellow patriots. Esther 5:14 states, "Let a gallows be made…and tomorrow speak unto the king that Mordecai may be hanged thereon…. And the thing pleased Haman; and he caused the gallows to be made."

Similarly, just as Haman was pleased, satan is pleased with himself and his accomplishments, but he still has one desire. This desire has become an obsession—to sit on the throne and be like God.

Satan had to leave the presence of the heavenly King to go back to his own turf (earth). Chapter 5 has set the stage for Almighty God to reveal His wonder-working power. The battle lines are drawn and the conflict is crystal clear.

Chapter 6

The Deceit of Pride

A Sleepless Night

Chapter 6 of Esther centers on the correction of an oversight by a benevolent and righteous ruler. This oversight is brought to light during a sleepless night. The cast of characters includes the king, Mordecai, the conspirators, and Esther. The dramatic action includes the oversight and, finally, a proper reward for Mordecai.

Esther 6:1-2

The king cannot sleep. Desiring to utilize this restless time efficiently, the king asks to have the court records read to him. He chooses to review the recent events and evaluate whether or not issues have been dealt with properly. As ruler and leader of the kingdom, his responsibility can be categorized under two headings: (a) staying abreast of all events, both local and foreign, and (b) administering justice.

The king faces a rude awakening. When the records are opened, he discovers that Mordecai has never been rewarded for uncovering an assassination plot. Mordecai had saved the king's life.

A closer look at this midnight scenario offers some pro-vocative insights, both intellectually and spiritually. Morde-cai had performed a loyal and noble deed, the exposure of a conspiracy to overthrow the king.

Mordecai is symbolic of Jesus the Living Word and His great deed. King Ahasuerus is symbolic of the Heavenly Sover-eign. The two conspirators, Bigthan and Teresh, are sym-bolic of the sinful, rebellious nature of man united with rebellious fallen angels (demons), working together to out-smart and overthrow the heavenly King. However, because the Living Word has positive, inside knowledge about the conspirators, He is able to inform His Church (Esther). He has enabled them to enter the throne room with petitions and information about existing situations.

Esther was given to Mordecai to be reared and nurtured. As a parallel, we see the heavenly Father giving Jesus the job of watching over, instructing, and directing His Church. John 6:39 states, "And this is the Father's will which hath sent Me, that of all which He hath given Me I should lose nothing, but should raise it up again at the last day." This as-sertion documents Jesus' commitment and empowering. He will keep and eventually resurrect His Church. John 17:9 continues, "I pray for them: I pray not for the world, but for them which Thou hast given Me; for they are Thine." This reveals Jesus' custodianship over those whom God declares are His. This extremely close-knit relationship between Je-sus and His Church is described even further in John 10:14: "I am the good shepherd, and know My sheep, and am known of Mine." John underscores this point in John 10:27 when he says, "My sheep hear My voice, and I know them, and they follow Me."

These Scriptures also describe the relationship between Mordecai and Esther. A watchful, caring, protective Mordecai shepherds an obedient, trusting, submissive Esther. The Lord Jesus, the Good Shepherd, is doing precisely the same for all those who have been given to Him by the heavenly Father of Might.

Esther 6:3

The story continues. The king inquires as to what reward has been given to this man Mordecai. The response is terse and sobering: "Nothing."

Has Jesus been fully rewarded for His matchless sacrifice at Golgotha, the greatest deed ever performed? In one loving act, the crucifixion, Christ not only exposed the evil workings of sin and satan, but He also destroyed the power of sin and satan. The evils of man's sinful nature and satan's seducing, perverted spirits were dealt a mortal blow.

Irritated by Jesus' message and challenged by His life and miracles, the sinful, proud, self-righteous nature of mankind cried out, "Kill Him!" Mankind believed that with His presence gone they could feel comfortable once again. However, Almighty God had different plans.

The resurrection of Jesus shattered the conspiracy generated by this evil combination. The Gospels have recorded evidence that details the teachings, the life, and the actions of Jesus. He allowed men to execute Him even though He had the power to escape out of their hands. His crucifixion and resurrection sent a message to the heavenly King that sinful men and rebellious spirits are at work trying to overthrow Him and all His laws and standards.

As Mordecai voluntarily exposed an evil plot, Jesus also, through His own willing sacrifice on the cross, exposed the absolute and ultimate workings of evil. What reward had

Mordecai received for His noble action? None. Yet in Esther 2:19 we read, "And when the virgins were gathered together the second time, then Mordecai sat in the king's gate."

Mordecai held a position he evidently received because of Queen Esther. Her newly acquired position and influence seems to have helped Mordecai attain his new status. No one knows precisely what this position was. It could have been a position responsible for security and maybe part of this responsibility was to screen all who might desire to have a meeting with the king. Surely anyone who had performed such an act of loyalty could be trusted.

Jesus has also been given a position by the heavenly King. What role is Jesus filling in this position? Colossians 3:1 says, "If ye then be risen with Christ, seek those things which are above, where Christ sitteth on the right hand of God." This right hand seat represents an influential seat of power, second only to the King's throne. First John 2:1 declares, "My little children, these things write I unto you, that ye sin not. And if any man sin, we have an advocate with the Father, Jesus Christ the righteous."

Sinful man cannot come near a holy God. God is an all-consuming fire when it comes to sin. Therefore, lest a man come to God and be destroyed, the mercy of God has placed a Man at His right hand to protect man, not God, from destruction. This truth is found in the Old Testament. God placed the mercy seat on the ark. It covered the tablets in the tabernacle for Israel's protection. The writer of Hebrews 10:12 states, "But this Man, after He had offered one sacrifice for sins for ever, sat down on the right hand of God." Jesus, through His voluntary sacrifice on the cross, exposed the absolute workings of evil. In this position He is to screen out all sinners who try to approach God inappropriately.

Yet His Word says that "whosoever will can come" (Mt. 10:32). What does Jesus mean by "whosoever" and "can come" (Mk. 8:34)? Who can come to God? The Bible is replete with answers to this question. Sin is a power that separates man and God. Is there an antidote, a remedy? Romans 3:23 states, "For all have sinned, and come short of the glory of God." Therefore, all men must be separated from God.

There is an inborn, eternal, conscious nature in mankind that cries out, "Who is God?" If I am *born* a sinner and am a sinner by *heredity*, then I am eternally damned from birth since God is holy and cannot abide or dwell where sin is. What a dilemma!

But wait! Holy Scripture declares, "...without shedding of blood is no remission" or removal of sin (Heb. 9:22). There is a remedy for this condition. This alone permits a Holy God and man (with his sin removed), to unite once again.

Whose blood is sufficient to accomplish such a wonder as this? First John 1:7 states, "But if we walk in the light, as He is in the light, we have fellowship one with another, and the blood of Jesus Christ His Son cleanseth us from all sin." This is the great deed performed for the King of Heaven. His Son voluntarily gave His life as a ransom for sin.

Parents can rear children and then allow them to be taken off to war by governments, all for the sake of so-called justifiable causes. When a son is lost at war, it is called a supreme sacrifice; but unfortunately, in time we are left wondering. Usually the accomplishments are very temporary and we question some of these sacrifices.

With Jesus, however, we are talking about a true, supreme sacrifice, made by only one Man. He alone was capable of performing this. Further, His sacrifice was not temporary, but eternal in its accomplishments. The only motivating power for this act was divine love. John 3:16 declares, "For God so loved the world, that He gave His only begotten Son, that whosoever believeth in Him should not perish, but have everlasting life." The Son so loved the Father that He was willing to lay down His life to become the blood sacrifice.

Anyone who accepts this truth is guaranteed eternal life. All that is necessary is an acknowledgment to the heavenly King of one's sin nature and a declaration that Jesus the Christ died for him/her personally. This truth can be applied even at this very moment, and a liberation can be experienced.

John 14:6 states, "Jesus saith unto him, I am the way, the truth, and the life: no man cometh unto the Father [heavenly King], but by Me." As Mordecai functions in the king's house in a position of trust and security, so Jesus Christ sits at God's right hand as God's highest security officer. He allows entrance only to those who have accepted the King's rules and have received clearance. Unrepentant sinners are not allowed.

Hebrews 9:11–12,25 establishes this truth:

But Christ being come an high priest of good things to come, by a greater and more perfect tabernacle, not made with hands, that is to say, not of this building; Neither by the blood of goats and calves, but by His own blood He entered in once into the holy place, having obtained eternal redemption for us … Nor yet that He should offer Himself often, as the high priest entereth into the holy place every year with blood of others (Hebrews 9:11–12,25).

Consequently, if you want visitation rights, obey the heavenly King's rules. Get rid of your sins by confessing them properly and sincerely. Hebrews 10:21–22 declares, "And having an high priest over the house of God; let us draw near with a true heart in full assurance of faith, having our hearts sprinkled from an evil conscience, and our bodies washed with pure water."

Honor Long Due

Esther 6:4

Haman's wrath turns to fury because Mordecai, now seated within the king's council room, refuses to stand at Haman's presence. This act of refusing to stand, coupled with his act of refusing to bow, ultimately pushes Haman into his course of action. Haman intends to destroy Mordecai. He has already been plotting Mordecai's destruction by designing and constructing a gallows (75 feet high) in his own front yard. He intends for Mordecai's death to be public and conspicuous.

Gallows were usually constructed on platforms with stairs leading up, and were called scaffolds. We can visualize this construction of platform upon platform, staircase to staircase, to a height of 75 feet. Viewers could only ask, "What is this?" Even those who took part in the construction did not know its ultimate purpose. Only as the last platform was put in place and the hangman's noose readied from the support beam could one understand the construction.

On earth Jesus Christ the Living Word did not bow down nor submit to satan's lying tactics, his subtle maneuvering, nor his pretension to equality with God. Now as the Living Word seated at the right hand of God, He intercedes only for those who submit themselves to God's laws and who accept the only means of redemption, the atoning blood of the Lamb of God (Jesus). To those alone He pays attention.

Satan continually goes before God with false accusations against believers, bending the truth, trying to get a consuming God to act in judgment against them. The Interceding One is seated at the right hand of the Father, the seat of shared authority. As the Advocate before the Father, He is occupied with fulfilling His many promises to His children. He ignores satan, figuratively speaking, by refusing to stand (a posture that acknowledges one's recognition of) and thereby diverts any attention to and refuses to exhibit the least interest in satan's continuous slanderous activity. Satan hates Jesus. He will try to attack, destroy, and annihilate anyone who has a relationship with Jesus the Living Word.

Esther 6:5

Haman, standing in the king's inner court, with the gallows already built, is ready to execute his plans. At this precise moment King Ahasuerus is getting ready to reward Mordecai (Haman's hated enemy) fully for his loyalty. Standing before the king, Haman is filled with pride at his accomplishments and is concerned for his own glory. The king asks him for ways to honor someone who has delighted him with loyalty and courage. In the blindness of his proud heart, Haman visualizes himself as the recipient of this honor. He has dreams of being king, or at least being equal to the king. The dialogue between the king and Haman, as recorded, vibrates with dramatic irony. Haman comes to get permission to hang Mordecai and proposes honors he covets for himself, only to find them given to the very man he wishes to destroy!

So Haman came in. And the king said unto him, What shall be done unto the man whom the king delighteth to honour? Now Haman thought in his heart, To whom would the king delight to do honour more than to myself? And Haman answered the king, For the man whom the king delighteth to honour, let the royal apparel be brought which the king useth to wear, and the horse that the king rideth upon, and the crown royal which is set upon his head: and let this apparel and horse be delivered to the hand of one of the king's most noble princes, that they may array the man withal whom the king delighteth to honour, and bring him on horseback through the street of the city, and proclaim before him, thus shall it be done to the man whom the king delighteth to honour. Then the king said to Haman, Make haste, and take the apparel and the horse, as thou hast said, and do even so to Mordecai the Jew, that sitteth at the king's gate; let nothing fail of all that thou hast spoken (Esther 6:6–10).

Isn't Haman's dream the exact dream, desire, and proclamation of lucifer or satan? Isaiah 14:12–14 states:

How art thou fallen from heaven, O Lucifer, son of the morning! how art thou cut down to the ground, which didst weaken the nations! For thou hast said in thine heart, I will ascend into heaven; I will exalt my throne above the stars of God; I will sit also upon the mount of the congregation, in the sides of the

*north; I will ascend above the heights of the clouds; I
will be like the most High* (Isaiah 14:12–14).

Pride distorts. It bypasses the joy of true accomplish-
ment with exaggerations and vain imaginations that as-
sumes false things about one's own being and abilities.
Because of this distortion and blindness, pride becomes
oblivious to the obvious.

The power of hate plays a part in this blindness. Hate
prevents the pride-filled one from surrendering, even when
he knows he has lost. Hate pushes him to do as much dam-
age as possible despite certain defeat. Cruelty is born of hate
and seeks to destroy anything the opponent treasures.

So it is with satan. A created being can never be identical
to an eternal self-existing God. However, in the blindness of
pride, satan assumed he could be equivalent to the most high
God. When the Living Word, by His death and resurrection,
defeated satan, satan's fury focused upon destroying his opponent's treasure, God's people.

Just as Haman's gallows had been raised to defeat Mordecai, and the edict for the genocide of the Jews had gone
out, so the new world order is rising swiftly with its anti-
God message. It is being used by the satanic ruler of the end
times to try to eradicate the Living Word by destroying His
people (Judaic and Christian) who have put their faith and
trust in His Living Word.

The Living Word has made promises and is covenanted
to a nation called Israel, and also the Living Word has made
promises and is covenanted to a group of people called the
Church. The true representatives of both groups are the eternal stumbling stones for the god of this world and his vain
aspirations. Truly his is the ultimate vanity.

The true purposes of this new world order are cleverly camouflaged, just as Haman's elaborate gallows could have been mistaken for good intentions while under construction. Perhaps its builders, using the best of materials, unique designs, and top-notch craftsman, saw it as something of grandeur. The builders, because of their involvement, had now become accomplices to the fact.

To the unsuspecting, the new world order is advertised as man's only hope of survival. To the economically devastated, it preaches provision for every citizen of the world. To the sick, afflicted, and elderly, it preaches security. To the war-torn and weary, it presents the white dove of peace.

It promises to eliminate all social ills forever. Our streets will become crime free! It will minimize religious differences by emphasizing the goodness in all religions; accommodation or political correctness will be the bywords; unity the goal. With all of these promises, we must be entering a utopia, a period of peace and prosperity. Anyone who will not bow and submit to this order must be dealt with in a harsh and effective way.

There is another dimension of history unfolding relentlessly and on schedule. While the new world order, like Haman's scaffold, is rapidly taking shape, Jesus will arise from His seat as interceding High Priest to be rightly crowned. I believe the materialization of the new world order will, as it nears its completion, be the signal that releases the glorious moment when Christ receives His kingly robes, His kingly authority, His white horse, and the power which these regal appointments symbolize. Mordecai portrayed this scene perfectly.

Let the royal apparel be brought which the king useth
to wear, and the horse that the king rideth upon, and
the crown royal which is set upon his head: and let this
apparel and horse be delivered to the hand of one of
the king's most noble princes, that they may array the
man withal whom the king delighteth to honour, and
bring him on horseback through the street of the city,
and proclaim before him, Thus shall it be done to the
man whom the king delighteth to honour (Esther 6:8–9).

I believe this scene corresponds to the time when Christ will come for His Bride, prepared to receive this reward for His loyalty and faithfulness to His Father, the heavenly King. How soon? Just follow the daily events as they continue to materialize.

The important question is, "Whose side are you on?" Only you and I can make this decision. Vote for Mordecai. Choose Jesus the Christ. Become one of His people, one of those who are submissive to all that He speaks just as Esther was totally submissive to Mordecai. Jesus is soon to be rewarded and crowned King of the true new world order that will bring in the real utopia on earth.

Esther 6:12

A defeated, shocked, and humiliated Haman rushes home. He realizes that his very dreams have been awarded to his enemy.

Satan, the god of this world, will also scurry to regroup when he realizes the ramifications of the return of Jesus for His Bride and the inevitable heavenly coronation to follow. When Jesus is clothed in the garb signifying His full equality with the King, satan (who has been the accuser of the brethren before the throne of God), will realize that his demise, prophesied in Revelation 12:12, has taken place. "Therefore rejoice, ye heavens, and ye that dwell in them. Woe to the inhabiters of the earth and of the sea! For the devil is come down unto you, having great wrath, because he knoweth that he hath but a short time."

Esther 6:13

Chapter 6 ends on a dual note of panic and urgency. A trembling and frightened Haman listens with alarm to his wife's dour remark; Zeresh and the wise men inform Haman that if Mordecai is one of the seed of the Jews, Haman is guaranteed ultimate defeat. While they are still talking, the King's chamberlains apprehend him and quickly escort him to the second banquet Esther has requested.

To all who have dared to challenge God's authority, God promises a final crushing blow. Just as words of doom confronted Haman, satan heard God's proclamation in the Garden of Eden. God said that the seed of the woman would crush satan's head and ultimately destroy all his power (Gen. 3:15). Satan's final defeat would come from the seed of the woman. The seed was virgin born Immanuel. Immanuel means "God is with us" or "the Mighty One is here."

The promise of Genesis becomes more explicit in Isaiah 7:14: "Therefore the Lord Himself shall give you a sign; behold, a virgin shall conceive, and bear a son, and shall call His name Immanuel." Matthew 1:23 reveals how this was fulfilled. This same Immanuel, the Living Word, came to save His people and to destroy the enemy—the god of this world and his servants.

For the nonbeliever, this closing episode foreshadows frightening prophetic parallels. God's Word will be fulfilled swiftly and accurately, open to view for any who wish to make correct decisions. We are living in fast-moving times. The prophesied events of Scripture are closely guarded and administered. God declares in Jeremiah 1:12, "Then said the Lord unto me, Thou hast well seen: for I will hasten [watch over] My word to perform it." Examining God's Word in conjunction with historical events, everyone can see God's real drama unfold. God not only wants His people to observe the signs, but also to become responsive and get involved. *Truly, the time is short!*

Chapter 7

Evil Exposed

Esther's Petition Revealed

The reverses of the previous chapter initiated surprising shifts in the action of the drama. Consequently, a most fascinating scenario unfolds in chapter 7 as King Ahasuerus and Haman attend a second banquet given by Queen Esther. The previous day, risking her life, the queen entered the king's court with an agenda: She wanted to intercede for her people. However, when the king extended his scepter (in the gesture that overrode the penalty of death to any who entered uninvited), Esther made no request other than to ask the king to come that evening to a banquet she had prepared for him and Haman. She included a comment in the invitation. She wanted to wait until the following day to inform the king of her request.

Esther 7:1–3

Now, at the second banquet, the king prods Esther, "What is thy petition, Queen Esther? and it shall be granted thee, and what is thy request? and it shall be performed, even to the half of the kingdom" (Esther 7:2). In verse 3 Esther opens her response with the phrase, "If I have found favour in thy sight, O king" (Esther 7:3). Esther did everything possible to please the king. She came with a meek and humble spirit, one reflecting total submission to the king. These were attitudes that could only lead to a oneness of mind and heart. It is at this point Esther begins to reveal her petition.

Oneness of heart between the people and their King, just as seen in Esther, is something you can expect to see more pronounced among true Christians and faithful Jewish people. Indeed, I believe this is taking place all over the world. It is manifesting itself in local Christian gatherings, but the real evidence is in the personal lives of people as they adhere to the things God has called and instructed them to do individually. It has also been manifesting itself in the activities of the Jewish people for the past hundred plus years, and especially in more recent times with their return to the land of Israel. Their hearts are longing for peace and their Messiah. Both groups show evidence of a more visible oneness with God's Word.

By "Christian" we do not mean all that is labeled Christendom, nor by "Israel" every Jewish person from birth. The New Testament describes Christendom as a field filled with wheat and tares (Mt. 13:37-38). It illustrates a composite of faithful and masquerading believers. The Old Testament describes Israel as being comprised of a faithful remnant with many apostates. It is in the faithful remnant that a oneness or standing together is becoming more obvious (Joel 2:32).

Esther 7:3-6

Esther asks the king for his favor, and there is no implication that he will deny her request. Obviously, the offer he previously made, even to giving her half the kingdom, is still open. Now, the queen's heartache is about to be fully unveiled. It is clearly reflected in her countenance. In response to the king's question, Esther 7:6 records, "And Esther said, The adversary and enemy is this wicked Haman. Then Haman was afraid before the king and the queen."

Esther is representative of the Church, the group of people called out by the Spirit of God, and entrusted to Jesus the Living Word. Esther ultimately unveils Haman, the masquerading egotist, the perpetrator of evil in the Persian kingdom. In the same way, for 2,000 years the Church has been informing the throne of God with her prayers and petitions. These prayers have reflected all the things that have been causing a great disturbance to the Church—not only to her, but also to the Jewish people who have been prime targets for the god of this world system. First Peter 5:8 warns, "Be sober, be vigilant; because your adversary the devil, as a roaring lion, walketh about, seeking whom he may devour."

Haman: A Person and a Character Portrayal

Haman, whose name means "splendid," represents the epitome of pride. He thought of himself as splendid. The created angelic being, lucifer, was the first one in whom pride was found. The prophet Obadiah states, "The pride of thine heart hath deceived thee, thou that dwellest in the clefts of the rock, whose habitation is high; that saith in his heart, who shall bring me down to the ground?" (Obad. 3) Pride reveals itself in a smugness, a feeling of security based upon externals. It is a false security and all who dwell in it are guaranteed a casting down, whether individuals, nations, or groups; both angelic and human.

There is a guarantee in God's Word that He will utterly destroy pride. Self-admiration fails to realize that beauty and ability are gifts of God to be used for His glory. God's course of action is always appropriate. He alone is self-existing; no one existed before Him. All others are created beings and as such are dependent upon Him and are responsible to adhere to His laws. It is pride, with all its deceitful workings, that attempts to undermine the sovereignty of God through lies.

Not only will God destroy pride, but He will also destroy the one and only being who is responsible for its existence and promotion. Several references identify this being. Job 41:34 states, "He beholdeth all high things: he is a king over all the children of pride." Job 41:1 calls him "leviathan." In the Book of Revelation he is called "the dragon which gives power." Other descriptions include the serpent, the devil, the prince of the power of the atmosphere, the god of this world, the ruler of this world.

In the Book of Esther, Haman is a major representation of the actions of this being. The god of this world, pride personified, has been consistently at work to produce "this new world order." It has been incubating behind the scene, in the secrecy of darkness—something which only a few people (those who faithfully read and search God's Word) readily perceive and understand. It utilizes all the approaches and powers of this world's system. It is a product of lying, cheating, killing, bribery, and propaganda. It will use all these things to hinder or destroy anything that gets in its way.

The people who have subscribed to its dominion down through time have been nothing but dupes for the prince of this world. He has been at work, deceiving them into believing that what is becoming manifest is the glory of the one world government proclaimed in Scripture. This "new world order" has to be from hell because all the principles it uses are antagonistic to the characteristics of God, Christ, and His laws, as revealed through His Holy Scriptures.

The Mystery of Esther has been written because I believe that the Book of Esther, with many other Scriptures, is disclosing this very clearly. We are closing in on the time of God's coming judgments. God is merciful and long-suffering, but a time is coming when these qualities will, of necessity, yield to a holy anger in an awesome display of His justified fury. Mankind is being seduced and is yielding to the spirit of this world. This is especially true for many within the ranks of Christendom. Many by their lives are openly repudiating God's righteousness and love.

Comparisons and Instructions

As we saw at the end of chapter 4, Esther took two days to prepare before appearing before King Ahasuerus. She spent her time in fasting and prayer. This time reference, two days, takes on additional significance in the light of Second Peter 3:8, which says, "But, beloved, be not ignorant of this one thing, that one day is with the Lord as a thousand years, and a thousand years as one day." With this Scripture in mind, Esther's two days of preparation prior to appearing before King Ahasuerus correlate with an equivalent 2,000-year period of history, encompassing the era from the call of Abraham to the crucifixion of Jesus. Esther appeared before the king on the third day in her best attire. Jesus, in the third millennia of time from the call of Abraham, made His appearance before the heavenly throne, robed in righteousness in a resurrected body and represented the Church (the redeemed). As Esther's unscheduled appearance before the king signaled an important message, Christ's ascension before the throne of the heavenly King also carried a message.

On the third day Esther requested the king and Haman to attend the first of her two banquets. The first banquet day is equivalent to the time period that began with the ascension of Christ through to the year A.D. 1000. We are now living in the second thousand-year period, corresponding to Esther's second banqueting day. It was on this day that Esther made her disclosure of a great evil, the planned annihilation of her people, and the perpetrator of this evil.

At this point the story line carries an urgent prophetic message. Will the Church also make a full disclosure of evil and its perpetrator during this second thousand-year period? The Church has been promised a resurrected body (1 Cor. 15:51-53). She has also been promised that she will ascend into the heavens at the sound of the trumpet. Will this be the moment when, like Haman, satan is exposed and cast down from the position of power that he holds? The parallels are clearly defined. This event will surely transpire in the near future.

After Esther's days of preparation and her entrance before the king, she was a hostess for two days. Haman, too, had been quite busy, activating his evil plan against Mordecai and for the genocide of the Jewish people. In the same manner, the false god of this world has activated his scribes and couriers.

Down through history, the Jews have been the targets of individual as well as collective holocausts. As it was throughout the Persian kingdom, so it has been worldwide in this A.D. time frame. The message delivered is clear and constant. It never veers off course. Its intent is one of annihilation. Its perpetrator is the god of this world, the anti-God spirit or antichrist spirit. Its operation is called anti-Semitism. As Mordecai acted to alert Esther in his day, so Jesus the Living Word is busily informing the true Church, "the called-out ones," and designating a people who, in obedience, have responded to God's message. There is a very enlightening, informative, and instructive Scripture, quite appropriate for this present time. It is only one of many messages that the Living Word is speaking to His called-out ones:

> *Comfort ye, comfort ye My people, saith your God. Speak ye comfortably to Jerusalem, and cry unto her, that her warfare is accomplished, that her iniquity is pardoned: for she hath received of the Lord's hand double for all her sins* (Isaiah 40:1-2).

Psalm 122:6 states, "Pray for the peace of Jerusalem: they shall prosper that love thee." These are only two Scriptures in reference to this matter. God's Word is filled with His intentions and His people are obligated to become informed and active.

As Haman went into action, so did Mordecai. He obtained Esther's attention, convinced her, and received an affirmative response. Likewise the Church, since her inception, has been informed of the evil intents and the workings of satan. This knowledge brings heaviness to one's spirit and sadness to one's countenance. This has been reflected for the past 2,000 years as the Church has gone before the heavenly throne with her prayerful petitions. The heavenly Sovereign's desire is to please all those who have come to Him with a submissive, obedient spirit to His will.

The major portion of the history of Israel as a nation has been one of misery and bondage. She has lived under four

Gentile powers: Babylonian, Persian, Grecian, and Roman, and has been scattered into all the nations. While under the Roman Empire, the last domination, the Jews were also under the dominance of the Sanhedrin and two major religious systems, the Pharisees and the Sadducees. All these major factions controlled them with bondage and heavy commitments. An admonition and invitation to God's wandering people, the nation of Israel, is recorded in Hosea 6:1–2: "Come, and let us return unto the Lord, for He hath torn, and He will heal us; He hath smitten and He will bind us up. After two days will He revive us; in the third day He will raise us up, and we shall live in His sight."

The prophet Hosea promised that on the third day they were to be revived, restored to life. Truly, on the Day of Pentecost, God fulfilled this promise in an electrifying rebirth of the relationship between His people and their one and only God. He established this relationship with every Jew who personally submitted himself to God's final instructions as delivered by His only begotten Son. This invitation was given to all mankind—whosoever desired to respond. On the Day of Pentecost we see the fulfillment of this promise, but it was only the first stage. This was a renewal of relationship by an act of God called spiritual birth. The life that Adam lost for all mankind had been reclaimed by the second Adam, Jesus, God's eternal Son, who took on the robe of humanity. First Corinthians 15:44-45 explains this enigma:

It is sown a natural body; it is raised a spiritual body.
There is a natural body, and there is a spiritual body.
And so it is written, The first man Adam was made a

living soul; the last Adam was made a quickening spirit (1 Corinthians 15:44-45).

This is the life Jesus possessed and He declared it available to all men. On Pentecost, a new group of people called the Church, consisting mainly of Jews who accepted and believed, became God's new earthly representation on earth. The message of the gospel then went forth and was accepted by the Gentiles. Christianity became more associated with the Gentiles than the Jews. Does this mean God is finished with the nation of Israel, the other group with whom He had made solemn covenants? No! As a nation of people they were set aside only temporarily. In this we see the correspondence of Esther to the Jews. Esther's true identity as a Jewess was hidden from the Jews. She knew her heritage, but they were totally ignorant that one of their own was queen of the realm. Likewise, true believers in the God of Israel and the Messiah of Israel, Jesus the Living Word, are like Esther. They are, or should be, spiritually aware of their relationship with Israel. Both are creations of God. He is at work in both to fulfill His plans.

At the same time, Israel is blind to her connection with the Church, as noted in Romans 11:25: "For I would not, brethren, that ye should be ignorant of this mystery, lest ye should be wise in your own conceits; that blindness in part is happened to Israel, until the fulness of the Gentiles be come in."

We are now seeing the fullness of the Gentiles approaching. The return of the Jews to their promised land, as God declared in Jeremiah 29:14, is evidence of this: "...and I will gather you from all nations, and from all the places whither I have driven you, saith the Lord...." Joel 3:2 says, "I will also gather all nations, and will bring them down into the valley of Jehoshaphat, and will plead with them there for *My people* and for *My heritage Israel*, whom they have scattered among the nations, and parted My land." These are only two Scriptures relevant to God's gathering His people and the nations for His purposes.

There is also a second correlation between Esther's two days of preparation. This applies to the period of the Church, now approaching 2,000 years of history since the Day of Pentecost. What a glorious manifestation is pending! Here it is not the giving of life to spiritually dead people as with the first event. This time the dead in Christ and those who are alive when the trumpet sounds will be raised with glorified bodies as First Thessalonians 4:15–17 states:

> *For this we say unto you by the word of the Lord, that we which are alive and remain unto the coming of the Lord shall not prevent them which are asleep. For the Lord Himself shall descend from heaven with a shout, with the voice of the archangel, and with the trump of God: and the dead in Christ shall rise first: then we which are alive and remain shall be caught up together with them in the clouds, to meet the Lord in the air: and so shall we ever be with the Lord.*

Two thousand years ago a small remnant of Israel was waiting for the promised Messiah. There will only be a remnant or a small percent of humanity who, having heard the gospel message, will be alert and waiting. Esther, on the third day, made her entrance into the presence of King Ahasuerus. Even so the Church must be preparing herself, making sure her garments are clean. She is watching, but she is also actively preparing for her grand entrance before the heavenly Sovereign. This remnant is promised glorious things, but those who reject God's offer can expect the judgments of an angry God. He alone has the remedy, the gospel, and He has offered it freely for the eternal benefit of all, both Jew and Gentile. Still, He is rejected by countless numbers. This rejection will only engage His justifiable anger.

Exploring further parallels, Esther's banquet symbolizes the banquet table that Jesus identifies as representing that time and place when the King of the Universe and His queen (His redeemed ones) are together. The deceiving spirit is also present. He has been loose in the world and is allowed access to the inner court before the throne of God. Job 1:6 describes this: "Now there was a day when the sons of God came to present themselves before the Lord, and satan came also among them." This deceiving being is also identified as "the accuser of the brethren" in Revelation 12:10. "And I heard a loud voice saying in heaven, Now is come salvation, and strength, and the kingdom of our God, and the power of His Christ, for the accuser of our brethren is cast down, which accused them before our God day and night" (Rev. 12:10).

The scenes quoted here delineate the parallels between this renegade archangel and Haman. Haman roamed about Ahasuerus' kingdom just as the accuser has freely roamed. Haman demanded worship because he considered himself worthy of it. Lucifer's pride promoted schemes to appropriate men's submission and worship. Haman, getting all but Mordecai to pay him reverence, was determined to unseat and destroy Mordecai. The unveiling of Haman as the would-be destroyer of Esther and her people corresponds to that moment when the glorious Church, united with her Savior and robed in glorified bodies, will come before the King carrying a message: "This is the perpetrator of *evil* in Your *Kingdom* on earth against my people, the faithful of Israel."

When Anger Advances to Fury

Esther 7:7–8

The drama continues with the king angrily turning his back upon Haman and leaving momentarily as if to collect his thoughts. One can almost hear him wonder, "How could I, the king, ever have allowed such a being to be next in power to me?" The king returns to the banqueting hall, having processed his initial fury, only to find Haman trying to seduce Esther and win her favor. The account in Esther 7:7–8 reads: "And the king, arising from the banquet of wine in his wrath went into the palace garden; and Haman stood up to make request for his life to Esther the queen; for he saw that there was evil determined against him by the king. Then the king returned out of the palace garden into the place of the banquet of wine; and Haman was fallen upon the bed whereon Esther was. Then said the king, Will he force the queen also before me in the house?" After dealing with one stunning revelation, now Ahasuerus finds Haman imposing himself upon the queen—injury added to injury, fury on top of fury.

What does this disclose in the unfolding drama of God's revelation to man? This action in Esther depicts a time of separation for the king from Haman and Esther. On his return the king finds Haman trying to seduce Esther. This seductive activity can be observed throughout Christendom. The Hamanic spirit of this world is trying to obtain Christendom's favor, thinking he can obtain an extension or an appeasement of the judgment placed upon him. This is the last time that Haman is allowed to come into the court of the king.

The Scriptures cited earlier reveal that a time will come when satan is denied access to the throne room or inner court of God. Revelation 12:12a states, "Therefore rejoice, ye heavens, and ye that dwell in them." Esther's identification of Haman's insidious plot corresponds to an exposure of satan. It is the Church, in her glorified state before the King of the Universe, who affirms, "He is the man." This witness will terminate satan's access to the throne of God. At the moment when the Church stands before the King and makes this great evil known, the heavens will rejoice. Victory and deliverance will have come into the heavens plural—not only in the celestial heaven, but in the atmospheric heaven also.

At the same time, this separation of the king and Haman (the King of the Universe and satan), provokes this commentary in Revelation 12:12: "...Woe to the inhabiters of the earth and of the sea! for the devil is come down unto you, having great wrath, because he knoweth that he hath but a short time." What is it that will take place to manifest this anger on earth? If he is cast out of the heavens unto the earth, where is the only other place he can take up residency to express his lying, deceitful, and seductive ways?

To understand the dynamics of the story, it is essential to consider what brings God pleasure. Many Scriptures reveal, basically, man was created for God's good pleasure and His alone. Man was created a spirit being so that God, also a spirit being, could have an intimate relationship with him. Through this relationship God allows man to partake of His heart. His joys come when we obey, His grief when He is disappointed, His sorrow and heaviness of heart over the waywardness of man, and His anger at blatant sin and rebellion. In a sense, through this spiritual relationship, God cohabits with or has an intimate relationship with man. Having established the significance of man to God, it is easier to grasp the enormity of the next segment of the unfolding drama.

Esther 7:8

> The spotlight focuses upon Haman and his attempt to seduce Esther. He knows his life hangs in the balance and he sees that the only possibility of escape lies with Esther. He uses his deceptive and persuasive ways to try to force himself upon her and win a much-needed favor.

The seductive measures used by satan's New Age gurus are a visible counterpart of Esther's scenario, especially as they are applied in the Church (God's faithful). She has exposed him and made him accountable before the king. She appears now to be his only chance of survival. The Book of Revelation says that the devil was cast out unto the earth. Satan, in order to try and preserve himself, or at least delay his inevitable end, tries to get himself totally entwined with the Church, God's called-out representation of His power and glory. In a move to carry out his last malicious maneuver, he takes charge of men and nations by literally cohabiting with a man. This is a relationship that only God is supposed to have with man. (See Revelation 12:7-9.)

Just as Haman seals his doom by his seducing moves toward Esther, so satan visibly exposes himself by his action. When the antichrist steps into the temple and proclaims himself to be God, he initiates God's judgments. This will be satan's last and ultimate move using his end-time ruler, who is in charge of his new world order. His plans are to annihilate the Living Word and even the remembrance of the names of Jesus and Jehovah, the God of Israel. He has been trying to get rid of God's people (both faithful Jew and believing Christian), thinking he can obliterate *God's Holy Scriptures* and the *Living Word.* Satan's ultimate sin will arrive in bodily form. The antichrist, indwelt by satan himself as he stands in the temple, will believe that he has finally attained his goals just as Haman believed. The days of grace are over; no longer are there restraints hindering the judgments of a holy God.

Esther 7:9–10

The chapter ends with Haman hanging upon the gallows he had built for Mordecai (the man the king had honored for his loyalty). These gallows were to have carried out Haman's ultimate triumph. Now they are the very instrument of his own demise.

In the same way, satan's world order, intended to supplant God's position, will be destroyed instead. Revelation 11:15 records, "…The kingdoms of this world are become the kingdoms of our Lord, and of His Christ; and He shall reign forever and ever."

All of God's revelations to man are an extension of His love. His desire for man is real. These revelations are not merely words, but words backed by His unlimited power. God wants all people to choose correctly. He can only abide and function where truth is and everything that is not of the truth will ultimately be consumed by His fire.

God's Word, His Son, and His Holy Spirit have been given to all people, but man has to make the choice. There are no outside options; there are two Gods, one true and one false; two ways, one right and one wrong; two leaders; two paths; two objects, life or death. Choose life; Jesus is life. Joshua confronted the people of Israel with this choice.

And if it seem evil unto you to serve the Lord, choose you this day whom ye will serve; whether the gods which your fathers served that were on the other side of the flood [Red Sea], *or the gods of the Amorites, in whose land ye dwell: but as for me and my house, we will serve the Lord* (Joshua 24:15).

The Word of God addresses all men. There are people who willfully neglect it, thinking they have evaded the dilemma of choice. In so doing, they make a fatal choice. Willful neglect or evasion of knowledge (thinking we can capitalize on a plea of ignorance), often succeeds in evading penalties in this life, but not so with God.

God cannot be manipulated; He knows the difference between honest or premeditated ignorance. All things are a matter of life and death to Him. Man can become productive by receiving newness of life, which enables him to live according to God's laws and ways. (This is eternal life and enables man to continue on eternally with God in a new and glorious place.) The man who remains unproductive (even destructive) will suffer in a place where his destructive ways will be confined, a place of eternal torment.

If you are out of step with the true God, but were once in step, do as Hosea 6:1 declares: "Come, and let us return unto the Lord: for He hath torn and He will heal us...." Repent means to turn around or turn back, change your way of thinking. As long as we are breathing and His Spirit is speaking, we have the option to return. A time will come when God's

Spirit stops calling to man. Man will then function as an instrument in satan's hand if he rejects this call. We do not know when God's final invitation will be extended. God does not lie. He speaks through the prophet Isaiah and Solomon:

> *I also will choose their delusions, and will bring their fears upon them; because when I called, none did answer; when I spake, they did not hear: but they did evil before Mine eyes, and chose that in which I delighted not* (Isaiah 66:4).

> *Therefore will I number you to the sword, and ye shall all bow down to the slaughter: because when I called, ye did not answer; when I spake, ye did not hear; but did evil before Mine eyes, and did choose that wherein I delighted not* (Isaiah 65:12).

> *Because I have called, and ye refused; I have stretched out my hand* [Jesus is God's hand extended], *and no man regarded; but ye have set at nought all my counsel, and would none of my reproof: I also will laugh at your calamity; I will mock when your fear cometh* (Proverbs 1:24–26).

Consider these Scriptures seriously. People always get what is coming to them. Those who listen to counsel and take advice from sources other than the Word of God will be the recipients of the calamities described in these Scriptures.

When God calls for something, the best thing to do is to respond. He is King of Kings and Lord of all. God doesn't delight in darkness, in lies, or in anything that violates His laws. His first law proclaims that we should worship the Lord God and Him alone, and serve Him with all our mind, body, soul, and strength. God hates people who set up their own standards to try to please and reach Him, people who persistently choose other avenues than those He has specified. People who follow their own religious paths reject God's path of truth, or they are people who have never been exposed to His truth. When we see people full of fears, we see evidence of God's Word. He will bring their fears upon them because when He called, they would not answer.

Perfect love casts out all fear.

Herein is our love made perfect, that we may have boldness in the day of judgment: because as He is, so are we in this world. There is no fear in love; because fear hath torment. He that feareth is not made perfect in love (1 John 4:17–18).

God is love. Jesus is love. If God resides in your heart, and you are listening to and obeying His counsel and orders, there is no fear—guaranteed!

Chapter 8

Righteousness Crowned

New Owners and Just Authority

Esther 8:1-2

The order to execute Haman pacified the wrath of King Ahasuerus. The opening verses of chapter 8 disclose the transfer of power and property from Haman to Mordecai: "On that day did the king Ahasuerus give the house of Haman, the Jews' enemy unto Esther the queen. And Mordecai came before the king; for Esther had told what he was unto her [informed King Ahasuerus of her kinship to Mordecai] and the king took off his ring, which he had taken from Haman, and gave it unto Mordecai and Esther set Mordecai over the house of Haman."

Esther, depicting the Church, received Haman's property. This is also Scripture's promise to the Church, to receive custodianship of the earth once again. God had given it to Adam, but satan usurped dominion. However, because of the deeds of the Son of God (Jesus), the title has been reclaimed by the acts of a righteous and loyal Man.

Mordecai, symbolic of the Living Word, had already achieved one position in the kingdom. Now the king is given a new perspective regarding the bloodline relationship that existed between Esther and Mordecai. When God the Father sees the glorified Redeemer and the glorified redeemed ascended and united before Him, their kinship will be revealed.

The king takes off his ring, signifying authority (removed from Haman), and gives it to Mordecai. In the same vein, God is going to take the ring of authority (usurped from Adam) away from the god of this world, satan, and give it to His Son, who will rule the earth and its nations with a rod of iron. Revelation 11:15 shows a transfer of power from one kingdom to another: "And the seventh angel sounded and there were great voices in heaven, saying, The kingdoms of this world are become the kingdoms of our Lord, and of His Christ; and He shall reign forever and ever."

Mordecai's installation in the seat of authority (formerly occupied by Haman) did not automatically stop events which the Jews' enemy (Haman) had set in motion. True, the evils of Haman had been disclosed and were now public knowledge. The decision to administer punishment upon Haman, by the same means he had purposed to eliminate Mordecai, had been authorized. The dividing of the booty (Haman's house to Esther and Haman's title to Mordeai) had been proclaimed. Even though a new order had been given for Mordecai's authority, there was still a severe problem.

Similarly, the triumph of Jesus by His death and resurrection did not immediately terminate the effects of what satan had already set into motion on earth. In the heavenlies these things have been decided, but there is still trouble on earth. Haman's orders could not simply be stopped. They could not be altered. Isn't this the same situation found in the last book of the Bible, Revelation? Revelation is a picture of the end of time, the years known as the tribulation, with its woes, seals, and vials symbolic of specific judgments.

These judgments cannot be altered, but during the time of great trial, God will give Israel everything she needs to defend herself. I believe that as all the nations of the earth are gathering against her, God is already establishing everything she needs by calling her back to the land. This is giving her time to dig in, so to speak.

God has given clarity of insight and an ability to apply scientific and technological advances in every field to the Jewish mind. More than this, Israel has a God who has promised to send a righteous King to sit upon the throne. He has also promised that He Himself would defend Jerusalem. These are only a few of the promises given the children of Israel. Their God has always been truthful and faithful. God's Word has given them instructions from the throne of Heaven. When these instructions are faithfully obeyed, Israel will receive divine help. He is giving them a chance to prepare themselves even as the Jews of Haman's day were given sufficient time to make designated preparations for self-defense.

Likewise, the true Church should be fully aware of what satan has planned and set in motion for the people of Israel. The Church's attitude should be as Esther's: "For how can I endure to see the evil that shall come unto my people? or how can I endure to see the destruction of my kindred?" (Esther 8:6) Without the nation of Israel there never would have been a Church. We are definitely related because we are both referred to as nations of God's making.

Sovereign Rights

Esther 8:3-7

Once again Esther asks the king for his intervention in circumventing the evil set in motion by Haman. Once again, his initial response is to extend his scepter.

It is interesting to compare the definition of "scepter" used here in contrast with that of chapter 5. Here the Hebrew word is *shebet*, which translates as "a stick for punishing." Here Ahasuerus amplifies Esther's sharing of the king's power and authority. He gives her permission to punish her enemies, saying in Esther 8:8 to both Esther the queen and to Mordecai the Jew: "Write ye also for the Jews, as it liketh you, in the king's name, and seal it with the king's ring: for the writing which is written in the king's name, and sealed with the king's ring, may no man reverse."

The king continues to reiterate his support for both Esther and Mordecai and give further instructions. He informs his scribes to write a royal decree to the Jews, officials, governors, and princes of the 127 provinces stretching from India to Ethiopia. This decree gives the Jews permission to unite and defend their lives and property on one day in all the provinces; namely, upon the thirteenth day of the twelfth month known as Adar, the day Haman had set for the extinction of the Jews.

Haman's infamous decree has been effectively countered by the decree that Mordecai penned and sealed with the king's ring. The couriers race to deliver the new law throughout the land. Esther 8:15 states, "And Mordecai went out from the presence of the king in royal apparel of blue and white, and with a great crown of gold, and with a garment of fine linen and purple: and the city of Shushan rejoiced and was glad."

All of this speaks of the entrance of Jesus the Living Word in the midst of His people Israel, of *His acceptance by them*, and of Israel's gladness. In the description of Mordecai, each element has a significance revealed in God's established Word. The prayer shawl worn by the men of Israel was designed by God Himself. God's directions, recorded by Moses in Numbers 15:38-40 (NIV), read as follows:

Speak to the Israelites and say to them: "Throughout the generations to come you are to make tassels on the corners of your garments, with a blue cord on each tassel. You will have these tassels to look at so you will remember all the commandments of the Lord that you may obey them and not prostitute yourselves by going after the lusts of your own hearts and eyes. Then you will remember to obey all My commands and will be consecrated to your God. I am the Lord your God...

The colors of blue and white, found in the Jewish prayer shawl and in the flag of Israel, signify faith and consecration. The crown of gold represents authority. The fine linen stands for righteousness and the purple symbolizes royalty. Mordecai's royal attire symbolizes the acquisitions of Jesus the Living Word. The robes of the King who is to sit on David's throne signify His faith, consecration, authority, righteousness, and royalty.

Jesus' faith was tested and proven. Hebrews 4:15 witnesses: "For we have not an high priest which cannot be touched with the feeling of our infirmities; but was in all points tempted like as we are, yet without sin." Countless places in the Gospels, including Christ's own confession, verify the fact that everything He said and did was a result of His complete faith in His heavenly Father. He consecrated Himself for the sole purpose of fulfilling His heavenly Father's will. Hebrews 7:28 declares, "For the law maketh men high priests which have infirmity; but the word of the oath, which was since the law, maketh the Son, who is consecrated for evermore."

Mordecai was crowned with a great crown of gold, indicative of his newly acquired position of authority. Likewise Jesus was crowned, as noted in Revelation 14:14: "And I looked, and behold a white cloud, and upon the cloud one sat like unto the Son of man, having on His head a golden crown, and in His hand a sharp sickle." In Scripture, righteousness is defined as "one who has faith in God" (Rom. 4:3) even as Abraham. Second Peter 1:1 states, "...to them that have obtained like precious faith with us through the righteousness of God and our Saviour Jesus Christ."

The apostle John identified the symbolism of fine linen as righteousness. Revelation 1:13 says, "And in the midst of the seven candlesticks one like unto the Son of man, clothed with a garment down to the foot, and girt about the paps with a golden girdle." The English word *garment* (phonetically *Mowpha'ath*) is a rendition of the Hebrew which has these definitions: illuminative, to shine, and brilliance. Truly, Peter and John witnessed this on the Mount of Transfiguration. In Revelation 19:8 John says, "And to her was granted that she should be arrayed in fine linen, clean and white: for the fine linen is the righteousness of saints." From these Scriptures we clearly see that white, in all its brilliance, typifies righteousness and that both Jesus and the Church are arrayed in these garments.

Judges 8:26 reveals that purple is the color of kings. It is included in the list of spoils of war: "…beside ornaments, and collars, and purple raiment that was on the kings of Midian…." Mark 15:17-18 also reveals that purple is a color of royalty: "And they clothed Him with purple and platted a crown of thorns, and put it about His head, and began to salute Him, Hail King of the Jews!"

Furthermore, the triumph of Mordecai the Jew over his enemy had an effect upon the entire city, bringing light, gladness, joy, and honor. Jesus is also the bearer of light. He produces gladness, joy, and honor. John 8:12 establishes this fact: "Then spake Jesus again unto them, saying, I am the light of the world: he that followeth Me shall not walk in darkness, but shall have the light of life." Esther 8:16-17 comments, "The Jews had light, and gladness, and joy, and honour. And in every province, and in every city, whithersoever the king's commandment and his decree came, the Jews had joy and gladness, a feast and a good day."

God's Two Servant Nations

The New Testament speaks of Israel's partial blindness and of the restoration of her sight in the episode of the fig tree. The fig tree is an analogy used for Israel throughout the Bible. Mark 11:12–14,19–20 tells the story of Jesus looking for fruit on a fig tree. Finding none, He cursed the tree, which died in a day's time from the root upward. However, since its root did not fully die, in time it would grow again. With the fig tree analogy for Israel, Mark pictures Israel's isolation (or separation) from a clear knowledge of God's directives. However, at a specified time and because of the Church's intercession, Israel will receive light, characterized by joy and gladness.

Another analogy also speaks about Israel...the vine and grafted branches. She has been pruned out of God's active plans and purposes for a time. She will be restored, the true branches will grow again, and once again she will have that clear and visible role recorded in the Old Testament Scriptures. (See Romans 11:23-27.)

As already noted, the Book of Revelation speaks very clearly about the multitude that comes from every corner of the earth. These will come out of the great tribulation. God will be administering His judgments on earth, but His love and His mercy will be extended to His remnant people, Israel, in such obvious displays of power that many other people will also become believers. During the time of tribulation, many will find the true redemption story and accept it. John the apostle said in Revelation 7:9, "After this I beheld, and, lo, a great multitude, which no man could number, of all nations, and kindreds, and people, and tongues, stood before the throne, and before the Lamb, clothed with white robes, and palms in their hands." Further, Revelation 7:14 states, "And I said unto him, Sir, thou knowest. And he said to me, These are they which came out of great tribulation, and have washed their robes, and made them white in the blood of the Lamb."

Esther 8:17

The last segment of Esther 8:17 observes, "...the Jews had joy and gladness, a feast and a good day. And many of the people of the land became Jews; for the fear of the Jews fell upon them."

The word *Jew* as defined in Scripture and used by Jesus meant "a true believer in God." Abraham was not a Jew simply because he was born physically of Jewish parents. The term "Jew" had not come into use yet. He was the first Jew, however, because he was called "the father of faith." For ensuing generations, physical birth has been a part, but not the most important part, of being Jewish. It was the faith that these people had in their God that made them true Jews.

In Romans 2:28–29, the writer comments, "For he is not a Jew, which is one outwardly; neither is that circumcision, which is outward in the flesh: but he is a Jew, which is one inwardly; and circumcision is that of the heart, in the spirit, and not in the letter; whose praise is not of men, but of God." This definition specifies an inward action or decision rather than human birth as the qualification that God recognizes for a Jew.

The word *intercession* incorporates representation; that representation may be carried out from a distance or by a personal appearance. The true Church, since her inception, has been carrying out her duties of intercession through prayer. But Scripture declares that one day the Church will make a personal appearance in her glorified state before the very throne of God (1 Thess. 4:13-18). This advent, known as the Rapture of the Church, will definitely mark a specific time in Israel's history. It will be the moment when she finally receives the light of her true God.

Both of these word pictures declare that God's Kingdom will finally be fully established on earth, in His way and in His time. His Word provides multiple references such as these. We can watch the development of the world government which shall appear (as previously alluded to in *The*

Mystery of Esther). We can positively distinguish the difference between satan's "new world order," and that which God has promised. Yes, we can watch and observe this order and its operation. It is because God, who knows the end from the beginning, is good and loving. He has shared this knowledge with us. He wants men to choose correctly and become involved in the development of His plans for His New World Order, for there is work to be done.

In whose world order are you involved? Souls must be saved. These souls will become the citizens of His new Kingdom. At one time America was perceived as a paradise for weary people in bondage to the humanistic political and religious systems that plagued mankind. America was the land of opportunity, the land of plenty, and the land of freedom. America was also a nation where every citizen had a right to voice his ideas in the political structure and operation of his nation. She also presented freedom for all who adhered to a faith and wanted to worship freely. She represented freedom to choose a life's vocation. Sadly, that portrait has become tarnished, just as other utopian dreams have faded.

The only true glorious message is that of God's soon-coming Kingdom described throughout Scripture, a kingdom of peace, justice, and sufficiency. Unregenerate leadership cannot produce or attain this. Only the Living Word, coupled with the true Church, will be able to bring this about.

Watch and work. Enlist. Become active. Become a part of His plans. Once again we repeat, man doesn't have to wait for dire times to act upon God's invitation (given in Revelation 3:20) to accept the Savior:

Behold, I stand at the door, and knock: if any man hear My voice, and open the door, I will come in to him, and will sup with him, and he with Me (Revelation 3:20).

Chapter 9

The Tables Turned

Sudden and Shocking Reverses

Chapter 9 covers D-day for the Jews, but instead of destruction, victory, celebrations and obligations are recorded. Utilizing Scriptures, history, and current events, we will expound on how this dramatized event will be carried out. Israel's ultimate D-day is on the horizon. A decree has been formulated by the Haman of this world, satan, to destroy the Jewish race. People have been trying to execute this decree and God in Heaven, the almighty sovereign God, has allowed some of this to happen. This consistently raises the question, "How can an all-knowing, good God allow such actions?"

The God of the Bible is a God bound to His Word. This is portrayed in the drama by the Persian king who is bound to his word. The fact that King Ahasuerus allowed such a decree to be passed can only be attributed to his being duped by the second most powerful person in his empire. Can we say this of God? An omniscient God was duped? Preposterous! Whatever questions human beings might have, the truthful answers can and will be found by those who look for them. God promises in Matthew 7:7, "Seek and ye shall find."

The very character and nature of God is "holiness." The word itself means to be "other," and as such, is unable to be equated with anything else that is. The word's meaning incorporates harmony in that all functions in perfectness. As we observe the world we live in, all is tainted and destined for death. From this standpoint, God cannot be equated with anything we know.

Perfection, harmony, peace, agreement, smoothness, and a multiplied number of other adjectives only begin to isolate the essence of "holiness." A challenge to God and the established laws of His universe swaggered into this perfection. This challenge wrapped itself in two truths in an attempt to thwart God's perfect purposes.

The first preyed upon God's design, His giving angelic beings and mankind the power of choice. The second wrestled with the character and nature of God. If bound only by the characteristics of His holiness and justice, He would have annihilated creation. But His nature, which also includes love and mercy, designed and implemented a plan for restoration. This created a situation whereby God was obligated to allow certain things to happen and also to continue.

These are the things we call "evil." Because God is who and what He is, He must step aside and allow evil to be operable for a season. He is not only a good and loving God, but also a holy and just God. He has to abide by His Word and stand behind what He has declared. Otherwise, He would not be the God that He has revealed Himself to be from the beginning of mankind's history.

From the call of Abraham, God revealed His person and plans to His people Israel. He provided a detailed record of His dealing with Israel in the Old Testament. Through His chosen leader and deliverer, Moses, God gave His message to His people Israel. He continued to amplify that message through His prophets, and finally culminated that message in His only begotten Son.

Throughout Scripture one quality alone dominates the description of God's dwelling place—holiness. Psalm 2:6 asserts, "Yet have I set My king upon My holy hill of Zion." David notes in Psalm 3:4, "I cried unto the Lord with my voice, and He heard me out of His holy hill." Again in Psalm 11:4 the proclamation affirms, "The Lord is in His holy temple, the Lord's throne is in heaven: His eyes behold, His eyelids try, the children of men." Another, Psalm 15:1, inquires, "Lord, who shall abide in Thy tabernacle? Who shall dwell in Thy holy hill?" Psalm 24:3 continues the question: "Who shall ascend into the hill of the Lord? or who shall stand in His holy place?"

These verses speak clearly and distinguish God's place of residence as holy. Further, Scripture delineates particularities of His holiness. Psalm 16:10 observes, "For Thou wilt not leave my soul in hell; neither wilt Thou suffer Thine Holy One to see corruption." Again, Psalm 22:3 says, "But Thou art holy, O Thou that inhabitest the praises of Israel."

God's name in itself is characterized as holy in Psalm 33:21: "For our heart shall rejoice in Him, because we have trusted in His holy name." Psalm 51:11 establishes this quality within His spirit: "Cast me not away from Thy presence; and take not Thy holy spirit from me." Psalm 99:9 reiterates, "Exalt the Lord our God, and worship at His holy hill; for the Lord our God is holy." His residence is holy and even His very name is holy; even His Spirit is holy.

There is a particular One called "The Holy One of Israel." How could this holy being called God allow such evil to take place on His created earth? How could He also allow Israel, His chosen people, to suffer as she has throughout history and during the present time? Daily we hear of attacks upon Jews, both individually and collectively, locally and worldwide.

The only true and appropriate answers spring from the Scriptures. Not only are they satisfactory answers, but they are also instructive. Not one of God's created beings is an idle spectator. Whether enlightened or darkened, each created being is always functional and a partaker of something. Each human being must make a choice. He may choose to follow the One who is truly splendid or the one who only *thinks* he is splendid.

Scriptures inform us that man was originally formed by God and that man was splendid like God (Gen. 1:26). But through disobedience, man lost his original splendor (Gen. 2:17). This original splendor was manifested through his obedience to his Creator's laws and the utilization of his God-given abilities.

Man now pacifies himself with his own limited achievements, deluding himself to believe that he has the potential to attain godhood. However, Scriptures proclaim that man was created *only* in God's image or likeness (Gen. 1:26). The lying spirit of this world capitalizes upon this delusion. He, through darkened leaders, tries to carry out this illusion through the new world order, humanism, New Age, and other similar groups.

This lying spirit utilizes the policies of political correctness and situational ethics to accomplish this delusion status of godhood, all espousing the same lie. Man can choose to believe the spirit of this world and be deluded, or he can believe the truth declared about himself in the Holy Scriptures. He can recognize that only God the Father, His Son, and His Holy Spirit are truly splendid and the only Ones that godhood pertains to.

Esther's story is larger than the actual historical events that it records. King Ahasuerus and Haman depict God and satan, a supreme being who permits and a secondary being who advocates a horrible decree. Unless something miraculous takes place, genocide will result. As the story recorded in Esther reveals, the miracle does take place. Therefore, we anticipate the same in soon-coming events. One day we will call these events "history."

Miracles or the benefical supernatural works of God are classified as blessings of God and are dependent upon faith. Faith frees God to administer these blessings. Faith is dependent upon God's light or knowledge. It is activated by obedience, for without faith it is impossible to please Him (Heb. 11:6). When God speaks the word *obey*, it is accompanied by specific instructions. When individuals or groups of people heed His command, they are guaranteed absolute blessing from an absolute God. The God of the Scriptures, the God of Israel, is the God of all people who will put their faith and trust in Him. He will truly bless their obedient response to His Word and Spirit.

Israel's day as a nation is coming, but the Word of God has mandated very specific responses to His Word before the ultimate blessing becomes theirs. Several references document the guaranteed promises. They are only attainable through obedience. Exodus 19:5 extends a promise: "Now, therefore, if ye will obey My voice indeed, and keep My covenant, then ye shall be a peculiar treasure unto Me above all people: for all the earth is Mine."

A message of instruction emerges in Exodus 23:23–25:

For Mine Angel shall go before thee, and bring thee in unto the Amorites, and the Hittites, and the Perizzites, and the Canaanites, the Hivites, and the Jebusites: and I will cut them off. Thou shalt not bow down to their gods, nor serve them, nor do after their works: but thou shalt utterly overthrow them, and quite break down their images. And ye shall serve the Lord your God, and He shall bless thy bread, and thy water; and I will take sickness away from the midst of thee.

Deuteronomy 11:26–28 lists promises of blessing, the response of an ever-present, powerful God. His holiness requires obedience. This same passage asserts that rejection of God's commandments will bring cursing because a holy God cannot be near to or be a part of anything that is contrary to His spoken word:

Behold, I set before you this day a blessing and a curse; a blessing, if ye obey the commandments of the Lord your God, which I command you this day: and a curse, if ye will not obey the commandments of the Lord your God, but turn aside out of the way which I command you this day, to go after other gods, which ye have not known (Deuteronomy 11:26-28).

In Deuteronomy 28:58-68 God enunciates very explicit guarantees and the result of failure to obey His covenant with His people:

If thou wilt not observe to do all the words of this law that are written in this book, that thou mayest fear this glorious and fearful name, THE LORD THY GOD; then the Lord will make thy plagues wonderful, and the plagues of thy seed, even great plagues, and of long continuance, and sore sicknesses, and of long continuance. Moreover He will bring upon thee all the diseases of Egypt, which thou wast afraid of; and they shall cleave unto thee. Also every sickness, and every plague, which is not written in the book of this law, them will the Lord bring upon thee, until thou be destroyed. And ye shall be left few in number, whereas ye were as the stars of heaven for multitude; because thou wouldest not obey the voice of the Lord thy God. And it shall come to pass, that as the Lord rejoiced over you to do you good, and to multiply you; so the Lord will rejoice over you to destroy you, and to bring you to nought; and ye shall be plucked from off the land wither thou goest to possess it. And the Lord shall scatter thee among all people, from the one end of the earth even unto the other; and there thou shalt serve other gods, which neither thou nor thy fathers have known, even wood and stone. And among these nations shalt thou find no ease, neither shall the sole of thy foot have rest: but the Lord shall give thee there a trembling heart, and failing of eyes, and sorrow of mind: And thy life shall hang in doubt before thee; and thou shalt fear day and night, and shalt have none assurance of thy life. In the morning thou shalt say, Would God it were even! and at even thou shalt say, Would God it were morning! For the fear of thine heart wherewith thou shalt fear, and for the sight of thine eyes which thou shalt see. And the Lord shall bring thee into Egypt again with ships, by the way whereof I spake unto thee, Thou shalt see it no more again; and there ye shall be sold unto your enemies for bondmen and bondwomen, and no man shall buy you (Deuteronomy 28:58-68).

The almighty God, always with His love, continues in Deuteronomy 30:1-20 with a plea to return to His covenant promises rather than face absolute destruction:

And it shall come to pass, when all these things are come upon thee, the blessing and the curse, which I have set before thee, and thou shalt call them to mind among all the nations, whither the Lord thy God hath driven thee, and shalt return unto the Lord thy God, and shalt obey His voice according to all that I command thee this day, thou and thy children, with all thine heart, and with all thy soul; that then the Lord thy God will turn thy captivity, and have compassion upon thee, and will return and gather thee from all the nations, whither the Lord thy God hath scattered thee. If any of thine be driven out unto the outmost parts of heaven, from thence will the Lord thy God gather thee, and from thence will He fetch thee: and the Lord thy God will bring thee into the land which thy fathers possessed, and thou shalt possess it; and He will do thee good, and multiply thee above thy fathers. And the Lord thy God will circumcise thine heart, and the heart of thy seed, to love the Lord thy God with all thine heart, and with all thy soul, that thou mayest live. And the Lord thy God will put all these curses upon thine enemies, and on them that hate thee, which persecuted thee. And thou shalt return and obey the voice of the Lord, and do all His commandments which I command thee this day. And the Lord thy God will make thee plenteous in every work of thine hand, in the fruit of thy body, and in the fruit of thy cattle, and in the fruit of thy land, for good: for the Lord will again rejoice over thee for good, as He rejoiced over thy fathers: If thou shalt hearken unto the voice of the Lord thy God, to keep His commandments and His statutes which are written in this book of the law, and if thou turn unto the Lord thy God with all thine heart, and with all thy soul. For this commandment which I command thee this day, it is not hidden from thee, neither is it far off. It is not in heaven, that thou shouldest say, Who shall go up for us to heaven, and bring it unto us, that we may hear it, and do it? Neither is it beyond the sea, that thou shouldest say, Who shall go over the sea for us, and bring it unto us, that we may hear it, and do it? But the word is very nigh unto thee, in thy mouth, and in thy heart, that thou mayest do it. See, I have set before thee this day life and good, and death and evil; In that I command thee this day to love the Lord thy God, to walk in His ways, and to keep His commandments and His statutes and His judgments, that thou mayest live and multiply, and the Lord thy God shall bless thee in the land whither thou goest to possess it. But if thine heart turn away, so that thou wilt not hear, but shalt be drawn away and worship other gods and serve them. I denounce unto you this day, that ye shall surely perish, and that ye shall not prolong your days upon the land, whither thou passest over Jordan to go to possess it. I call heaven and earth to record this day against you, that I have set before you life and death, blessing and cursing: therefore, choose life, that both thou and thy seed may live: that thou mayest love the Lord thy God, and that thou mayest obey His voice, and that thou mayest cleave unto Him: for He is thy life, and the length of thy days: that thou mayest dwell in the land which the Lord sware unto thy fathers, to Abraham, to Isaac, and to Jacob, to give them (Deuteronomy 30:1-20).

God's Plan Is on Schedule

Today Israel is faced with this ultimate declaration from God. Israel is returning, physically and spiritually, to her God. The false gods of this world are losing their hold. The hearts of Jews are yearning for their God and His promises as more and more nations close ranks against them. Scripture outlines the dilemma confronting Israel and God's role in their future. Joel 3:2 reveals God's heart for His people:

I will also gather all nations, and will bring them down into the valley of Jehoshaphat, and will plead with them there for My people and for My heritage, Israel, whom they have scattered among the nations, and have parted My land.

Zechariah 14:1-3 expounds upon the fate of Israel in a world hostile to them:

Behold, the day of the Lord cometh, and thy spoil shall be divided in the midst of thee. For I will gather all nations against Jerusalem to battle, and the city shall be taken, and the houses rifled, and the women ravished; and half of the city shall go forth into captivity, and the residue of the people shall not be cut off from the city. Then shall the Lord go forth and fight against those nations, as when He fought in the day of battle.

This latter reference reflects a parallel in modern history. The Jewish people began to come together at the turn of the century and now they are uniting and standing. Before, they moved from one nation to the next, seeking survival in what they might have considered to be safe havens. These havens may have been in any country initially offering an open door. At one point in time, they moved to new lands of discovery. Later on, they moved to nations that offered security through ideologies such as communism and democracy, but they never fully attained that safe place of complete peace and security.

The nation of Israel is now moving into a preparatory stance for the approaching day cited in Zechariah and Joel (see Zech. 14:1-4; Joel 3). A penetrating examination of the Jewish people (presently 4 million in the nation of Israel itself and 17 million plus worldwide) compared with all other peoples in the world (some 5.5 billion people), showcases a present-day people blessed by God with intellect, finances, and fortitude. In addition, God has used people in key positions of leadership to aid Israel.

Further, Israel possesses a strong military. Esther 9:2 testifies that "no man could withstand them." All men can verify that she is well armed and prepared today; yet these strengths alone will be insufficient to meet the days of trouble that lie ahead. However, Scriptures testify that she has a faithful and capable God at work in her behalf (Ps. 91). In this, we clearly see the blessings and promises of God.

Esther 9:3 says, "...the fear of Mordecai fell upon them." Just as Mordecai informed Esther, the Living Word of God reveals the very end from the beginning to those who want to know the truth. Scripture will do precisely this for those who will allow it to enlighten them.

An individual's fear or reverential awe of the Living Word (His person and His revelation in Scripture), will lead him to support God's people as He directs world events toward the day of Jacob's (Israel's) trouble. This day is quickly approaching. The first and best way to reach Israel is to declare the Word of God to the Jews. *Take the gospel to them.* As the apostle Paul said, "Preach the gospel to the Jew first."

Why first? When their religious and political leaders recognize Jesus as their promised Messiah, and they call for Him, then their final deliverance from their last and final challengers will take place. Zechariah 14:2-3 describes this:

For I will gather all nations against Jerusalem to battle; and the city shall be taken, and the houses rifled, and the women ravished; and half of the city shall go forth into captivity and the residue of the people shall not be cut off from the city. Then shall the Lord go forth and fight against those nations, as when He fought in the day of battle.

Only after God's proclaimed word is fulfilled will the King of Peace come back to earth and reign from David's throne.

Many Scriptures document clear identification of the Living Word as the Messiah or Anointed One for the Jewish people. Psalm 22:16 focuses upon the distinctive wounds left by the crucifixion of Christ: "For dogs have compassed me: the assembly of the wicked have enclosed me: they pierced my hands and my feet." Zechariah 13:6 adds, "And one shall say unto him, What are these wounds in thine hands? Then he shall answer, Those with which I was wounded in the house of my friends."

Then Zechariah 12:10 describes the meeting of the Jewish people with their promised Messiah:

And I will pour upon the house of David, and upon the inhabitants of Jerusalem, the spirit of grace and of supplications: and they shall look upon Me whom they have pierced, and they shall mourn for Him, as one mourneth for his only son, and shall be in bitterness for Him, as one that is in bitterness for His firstborn.

Finally, Zechariah 14:9 provides the final result of that meeting: "And the Lord shall be king over all the earth: in that day shall there be one Lord, and His name one."

These Scriptures reveal that in the last days all nations will come against Israel. However, there will be a people enlightened to God's truth who will be used in these final hours on Israel's behalf.

Esther 9:4 reveals the reason for the fear of Mordecai falling upon all the people as well as the officials: "For Mordecai was great in the king's house, and his fame went out throughout all the provinces: for this man Mordecai waxed greater and greater." The Living Word of God is becoming greater and more visible throughout the earth.

The Gospel of John tells of the Living Word incarnate. John 1:14 observes, "And the Word was made flesh, and dwelt among us, (and we beheld His glory, the glory as of the only begotten of the Father), full of grace and truth." The fame of Jesus of Nazareth and of His great deeds were common knowledge in His day. He gave Himself as a sacrifice for sin so all men could be cleansed. His sacrifice allowed God to take up residency in the place where He belonged from the beginning—within the hearts of individuals. This is God's house or dwelling place on earth. This group of individuals, the Church, has experienced expansion down through the centuries. The fame of Jesus, represented by Mordecai in the drama of Esther, increases exponentially on a daily basis. The Church is dynamically expanding throughout all the earth.

The destruction of individuals, nations, or systems who have hated the Jews has been evident throughout history.

This is powerful evidence of the truth of God's promise in Genesis 12:3: "And I will bless them that bless thee, and curse him that curseth thee: and in thee shall all families of the earth be blessed." The promise still stands.

Pride: Its Height and Depth

The final enemy of Israel will be satan's new world order, headed by the ultimate antichrist, represented by Haman. Haman was so obsessed with pride that he thought that all men should bow down to him, even Mordecai. However, God alone is eternal, powerful, and glorious and He alone deserves worship. All of creation should revere Him and Him alone.

Unfortunately, pride has the capability of deluding both angelic and human beings into thinking that God should become submissive to them. This is the apex of all that is called sin. Haman was steeped in the delusions of pride. So are the philosophies of the new world order. The names of Haman's ten sons are indicative of Haman's own character, as well as descriptive of the new world order. Although the etymology of two of the names has been obscured by time, the remaining eight provide pertinent insights:

1. *Parshandatha*—"Inquisitive." The ability to seek, to gain, and to retain knowledge. The power of computers, advancing continually, provides the end-time world order with astounding capabilities.

2. *Dalphon*—"The weeper." What Haman did (and what all those who side with him will do) when the king's new orders were proclaimed.

3. *Aspatha*—"The enticed gathered." All those who gave their allegiance to Haman because of the monies he had offered to accomplish his evil goal were gathered and destroyed—even his ten sons.

4. *Poratha*—"Bounteous." This incorporates the concept of having the power of riches at one's command. The United States enjoyed this position in the past. Will this continue or will this be shifted elsewhere in a rapidly-changing world?

5. *Adalia*—Unknown.

6. *Aridatha*—"Given by Hari." "Hari" is a Hindu word that translates to "a god" and also carries the force of thinking of oneself as a god. New Age thought promotes self-worship or worship of mankind as god, which will culminate in the incarnation of the serpent's seed. Genesis 3:15 documents that two seeds, two incarnations, will meet in battle. It states, *"And I* [God] *will put enmity between thee* [satan] *and the woman* [Israel], *and between thy seed* [the antichrist] *and her seed* [Jesus the Christ]; *it shall bruise thy* [satan's] *head, and thou shalt bruise his* [Jesus'] *heel.*

7. *Parmashta*—"Strong-fisted or strong willed." That which is imposed by force, both by military might and economic might. Daniel 8:23-25 and Daniel 11:36-39 describe such a situation taking place at the end of time:

And in the latter time of their kingdom, when the transgressors are come to the full, a king of fierce countenance and understanding dark sentences shall stand up. And his power shall be mighty, but not by his own power: and he shall destroy wonderfully, and shall prosper, and practise, and shall destroy the mighty and the holy people. And through his policy also he shall cause craft to prosper in his hand; and he shall magnify himself in his heart, and by peace shall destroy many; he shall also stand up against the Prince of princes; but he shall be broken without hand (Daniel 8:23-25).

And the king shall do according to his will; and he shall exalt himself, and magnify himself above every god, and shall speak marvellous things against the God of gods, and shall prosper till the indignation be accomplished: for that that is determined shall be done. Neither shall he regard the God of his fathers, nor the desire of women, nor regard any god: for he shall magnify himself above all. But in his estate shall he honor the God of forces, and a god whom his father knew not shall he honour with gold, and silver, and with precious stones, and pleasant things. Thus shall he do in the most strong holds with a strange god, whom he shall acknowledge and increase with glory: and he shall cause them to rule over many, and shall divide the land for gain (Daniel 11:36-39).

Daniel was so affected by this vision that he fainted and became ill.

A contemporary writer, Professor Carrol Quigly, authored a history book about man from his earliest recorded beginnings until the present time. Its message corroborates Daniel's vision of a political system with power at the end of time. Quigly's book describes a so-called inconspicuous political body that is in existence and functioning. He also asserted that nothing will be able to hinder its progress or stop it. He titled his work *Tragedy and Hope,* a curious name for a history book. In response to questions about his choice of this title, he responded that the tragedy was the birth of this pseudo political body which would function so flawlessly and that the only hope mankind had was to surrender to it.

What a description of satan's final world order, a system in absolute rebellion against God. This new world order will be presented in such a way that those who are not enlightened by God's true Word will accept the system as God-inspired, believing it will establish the long-desired utopia on earth. This will bring the world into the final stages in which satan and man are allowed to do things their way, a way which can only lead to destruction. With these objectives attained, satan will think himself equal to God and demand worship.

To travel the path of destruction means rejecting the true God, abandoning His guidance system, and to accept a pretentious, false system led by the antichrist.

However, only Jesus Christ is equal to God. When Jesus was baptized by John, God said, "This is My beloved Son in whom I am well pleased" (Mt. 3:17b). Luke 3:22 confirms Matthew's account: "...and a voice came from heaven, which said, Thou art My beloved Son; in Thee I am well pleased." On another occasion, Jesus took Peter, James, and John apart into a high mountain, and Jesus was transfigured before them. They watched as He conversed with Elijah and Moses. Mark 9:7 records this event: "And there was a cloud that overshadowed them: and a voice came out of the cloud saying, This is My beloved Son: hear Him."

In addition to this affirmation of Sonship, Psalm 110:1 describes the Lord speaking unto David's Lord to come and sit at His right hand, a position that signifies a throne of equal power to the ruling Lord. The passage reads, "The Lord said unto my Lord, Sit thou at my right hand, until I make thine enemies thy footstool." Those who are unacquainted with these truths lack the antidote for the antichrist's lies.

8. *Arisai*—Unknown.

9. *Aridai*—"Delight of Hari." This name *Hari* again raises the rhetorical question, "Who is the delight of this false god but satan himself, incarnate in a man?" Satan's so-called masterpiece is the antichrist: Second Thessalonians 2:9 says, " Even him, whose coming is after the working of satan with all power and signs and lying wonders." However, God the true Spirit became incarnate through the virgin birth of Jesus Christ.

Those who subscribe to New Age beliefs are awaiting the arrival of their leader. He will be Hinduism's eighth reincarnation or the final avatar. He will be Islam's final prophet. Many Jews will accept him as their long-awaited Messiah. Men who are ignorant of God's truth will be duped by the golden tongue of a man proclaiming to be the sought-after one. They will accept a man who will seem to have the answers to mankind's escalating problems.

How did Germany, a so-called civilized Christian country, accept Hitler? In the same way, society, at the end of time, will accept someone who appears to have the answers for the situations at hand. However, the false messiah's "answers" will doom man.

10. *Vajezatha*—"Son of the Atmosphere." The name of Haman's last son is especially descriptive of antichrist, who will be the so-called seed of satan.

Note what Ephesians 2:2 says: "Wherein in time past you walked according to the course of this world, according to the prince of the power of the air, the spirit that now worketh in the children of disobedience." Note how satan is connected with the atmosphere in this passage.

A further identifying element springs from the promise in Genesis 3:14-15: "And the Lord God said unto the serpent, Because thou hast done this, thou art cursed above all cattle, and above every beast of the field; upon thy belly shalt thou go, and dust shalt thou eat all the days of thy life. And I will put enmity between thee and the women, and between thy seed and her seed; it shall bruise thy head, and thou shalt bruise his heel."

The sequence involves two seeds or offspring meeting. In the encounter, one will be bruised but the other will be totally crushed. What a picture of Christ, the seed of the divine God, entering earth through the nation Israel. His physical body was bruised by the crucifixion. Satan and his seed to come, the antichrist, will be totally crushed. God's Word promises the destruction of this world order, a system enslaving mankind.

The ultimate instrument for achieving compliance will be the power of economic threat. Survival in this new world order will necessitate the taking of a mark on the forehead or hand. This is spoken of in Revelation 19:20 and will bring doom to those who comply. Satan and his seed will suffer the same fate: "And the beast was taken, and with him the false prophet that wrought miracles before him, with which he deceived them that had received the mark of the beast, and them that worshipped his image. These both were cast alive into a lake of fire burning with brimstone" (Rev. 19:20).

A God Who Still Answers Petitions

The enemies of the Jews are defeated. Throughout the provinces and in the capital city of Shushan, the Jews smite all their enemies with the sword. Chapter 9 concludes with not only the hanging of Haman's ten sons, but also the total annihilation of all of their remaining enemies. In the same way, Christ will destroy, not only the new world order, but all of His enemies. What was intended to be a time of tragedy for the Jews will become a time of victory and celebration.

The Jewish race has been rescued. The intensity of the drama began in chapter 5 when Esther approached the royal throne in faith and touched the scepter, symbolic of power. From that day onward, Esther moved and spoke with boldness and power. Again in chapter 8 Esther petitioned the king on behalf of her people. Again the scepter was offered to her, and in faith she reached out and grasped it.

Esther 9:1–32

The power of the throne has authorized the Jews to prepare themselves for the inevitable, evil day of Haman's
edict. Esther and Mordecai have given orders to the Jews
in the king's name. Now, in chapter 9, Esther has ready access to the king and his continued immediacy of response
to her requests.

Esther and her people have total victory because they are
prepared and able to punish their enemies. Because of the
roles played by Mordecai and Esther in this drama, the
people experience a great deliverance. In order for future
generations to remember this glorious event, the Feast of
Purim is instituted.

*And Mordecai wrote these things, and sent letters
unto all the Jews that were in the provinces of the
king Ahasuerus, both nigh and far, to establish this
among them that they should keep the fourteenth day
of the month Adar, and the fifteenth day of the same,
yearly, as the days wherein the Jews rested from their
enemies, and the month which was turned unto them
from sorrow to joy, and from mourning into a good
day: that they should make them days of feasting and
joy, and of sending portions one to another, and gifts
to the poor. ...Because Haman the son of Hammedatha,
the Agagite, the enemy of all the Jews, had devised
against the Jews to destroy them, and had cast Pur, that
is, the lot, to consume them, and to destroy them....
Wherefore they called these days Purim after the name
of Pur...* (Esther 9:20-22,24,26).

The dramatic equivalents of the main characters, Mordecai and Esther, are the Living Word and the Church. Jesus the Living Word, through the working of the Holy
Spirit, is in an on-going relationship with the Church, His

flock of believers. What is the major thrust and theme of this communication? The Church, His Bride, is to be ready, to be watching, and to be working. Because of the cooperation between Christ and His followers, the Almighty (symbolized by King Ahasuerus), is going to be moved and He will grant permission for deliverance from the evil destructive workings of satan and his deceived followers. This deliverance will not only be for Israel, but for all of mankind.

Esther 9:25

Esther 9:25 declares that when Esther comes before the king, the tables are turned, so to speak. The account reads: "But when Esther came before the king, he commanded by letters that his [Haman's] wicked device, which he devised against the Jews, should return upon his own head, and that he and his sons should be hanged on the gallows."

When the glorified Church, robed in her immaculate garments, is raptured into the presence of the heavenly King, the new world order will be brought to an end by the installation of God's true New World Order. In the drama, Haman's instruments of destruction (gallows for Mordecai and an edict authorizing the annihilation of the rest of the Jews), were used against him and his cohorts. Likewise satan, along with the device through which he is working, will be destroyed. His methodical annihilation of those who refuse to submit to him, in the guise of the new world order, will end.

Mordecai commanded the Jews to set aside two days, known as Purim, to observe the miracle of deliverance that had taken place. Perhaps the people of God will be celebrating two events. One event is already in place. The Lord's supper is a commemoration of the victory of the Living Word bringing deliverance from sin. Jesus became God's unblemished Lamb and then a perfect sacrifice. He sets all men who will receive Him free from the power of sin. Those who choose to believe and receive His forgiveness partake of His eternal spirit and the life which Jesus promised.

The second event may be the believers' exchanging mortal bodies for new glorified ones. The first event provided us with an eternal relationship by giving us eternal life through the power of His eternal Spirit. The other will provide an additional dimension, an eternal existence in a glorified body!

These are Scriptures that declare Christ's first position in the seat at the right hand of God just as Mordecai received a seat in the kingdom. Psalm 110:1 says, "The Lord said unto my Lord, Sit Thou at My right hand until I make Thine enemies Thy footstool." Hebrews 1:3 states, "Who being the brightness of His glory, and the express image of His person, and upholding all things by the word of His power, sat down on the right hand of the Majesty on high."

These Scriptures symbolize the time of King Ahasuerus' coronation of Mordecai. Mordecai had been given full authority before the Jews' final consummate victory over their enemies had taken place. Esther 9:29 states, "Then Esther the queen, the daughter of Abihail, and Mordecai the Jew, wrote with all authority...." This verse can be paraphrased as follows: "Then the Church, the heavenly Bride, the daughter of the 'Father of Might' and the Living Word, Jesus the Jew, the faithful Son who trusted His God and Father completely, are united and ruling together."

The joint endeavor and sharing of ruling power as perceived in that Scripture can be witnessed in the following one, Revelation 5:10: "And [Thou] has made us unto our God kings and priests: and we shall reign on the earth." Revelation 20:6 says, "Blessed and holy is he that hath part in the first resurrection: on such the second death hath no power, but they shall be priests of God and of Christ, and shall reign with Him a thousand years." Revelation 22:5 says, "And there shall be no night there, and they need no candle, neither light of the sun, for the Lord God giveth them light and they shall reign for ever and ever." First Corinthians 15:25 states, "For He must reign, till He hath put all enemies under His feet." Esther 9:30–31 reads, "And he [Mordecai] sent the letters unto all the Jews, to the hundred twenty and seven provinces of the kingdom of Ahasuerus, with words of peace and truth, to confirm these days of Purim in their times appointed...."

When this kingdom is finally established, then the world will truly know what the words *peace* and *truth* mean in verse 30. Mordecai could have been classified as a prince of peace for what he accomplished for the inhabitants of the Persian Empire, especially the Jews.

Jesus is the Prince of Peace as described in Isaiah 9:6: "For unto us a child is born, unto us a son is given: and the government shall be upon His shoulder: and His name shall be called Wonderful, Counsellor, The mighty God, The everlasting Father, The Prince of Peace." He alone can justly bear these titles because He alone possesses proper and sufficient power to establish true and everlasting peace. Further, He is truth personified, for He is God incarnate. Isaiah 7:14 says, "Therefore the Lord Himself shall give you a sign; Behold, a virgin shall conceive, and bear a son, and shall call His name Immanuel."

Ultimately, Jesus will again be back on earth, invited by His people Israel. The account given in Zechariah 13:8-9 alludes to the distress that prompts that invitation:

And it shall come to pass, that in all the land, saith the Lord, two parts therein shall be cut off and die, but the third shall be left therein. And I will bring the third part through the fire, and will refine them as silver is refined, and will try them as gold is tried: they shall call on My name, and I will hear them: I will say, It is My people: and they shall say, The Lord is my God (Zechariah 13:8-9).

The result of Israel's final fiery furnace is the destruction of two-thirds of the nation, but the purification of one-third who call on the Name above all names. What is the name they will use that will make God respond and say, "I will hear them"? The name is "Jesus."

Romans 10:1 says, "Brethren, my heart's desire and prayer to God for the Israelites is, that they may be saved." This verse was written by Paul, a very religious Jewish lawyer, one of the Sanhedrin, who had a personal encounter with the resurrected Jesus.

Like the writer of Romans, all true believers, those having had an encounter with this Christ, should share this cry. If not, then they are not true believers or they are poorly informed ones. Peace for this world hinges upon the return of Christ, the Prince of Peace; His return hinges upon His being issued an invitation to do so, a call from His brethren, the house of Israel. This won't take place until this truth is made real to Israel.

Satan has, in his deceitful ways, used ignorant and false Christians to carry out hideous crimes against the Jews. This has created a stigma between Jews and the name of Jesus. Acts 2:21 states, "...whosoever shall call on the name of the Lord shall be saved." Acts 4:12 (NIV) clarifies the process: "Salvation is found in no one else, for there is no other name [Jesus] under heaven given to men by which we must be saved."

Throughout the Bible, names have significant meanings. The name Immanuel means "the Mighty One is with us." Jesus or *Yeshua* means "Jehovah is our Salvation." Jehovah means "the eternal one who reveals Himself."

Matthew 1:23,25 records, "Behold a virgin shall be with child, and shall bring forth a son, and they shall call His name Emmanuel, which being interpreted is, God with us. ... And [Joseph] knew her not till she had brought forth her firstborn son: and he called His name Jesus."

From these definitions and recorded Scriptures, we clearly see the names given to the Son of God. He is the Mighty One sent from God with an eternal nature to be Israel's and mankind's only Savior. *He is the Lord Jesus Christ.*

Chapter 10

Rightful Recognition at Last

New Laws

Esther 10:1

"And the king Ahasuerus laid a tribute upon the land, and upon the isles of the sea" (Esther 10:1). The king places a tax upon the people, something which the citizens are compelled to pay.

Is something going to be placed upon the inhabitants of earth when the god of this world, satan, is replaced by a new ruler from Heaven? It is not going to be compulsory taxes, but it will be a compulsory yearly duty with dire consequences if not obeyed.

And it shall come to pass that everyone that is left of all nations which came against Jerusalem shall even go up from year to year to worship the King, the Lord of Hosts [the Eternal One], *and to keep the feast of tabernacles. And it shall be, that whoso will not come up of all the families of the earth unto Jerusalem to worship the King, the Lord of hosts, even upon them shall be no rain* (Zechariah 14:16–17).

It's All Been Recorded

Esther 10:2

"And all the acts of his power and of his might, and the declaration of the greatness of Mordecai, whereunto the king advanced him, are they not written in the book of the chronicles of the kings of Media and Persia?" (Esther 10:2)

John 21:25 notes the parallel between Mordecai and Jesus: "And there are also many other things which Jesus did, the which, if they should be written every one, I suppose that even the world itself could not contain the books that should be written. Amen." The deeds of Jesus, the Living Word, recorded in the Gospels, are only a small portion of all that He actually said and did. Jesus, the Living Word, promised, "For where two or three are gathered in My name, there am I in the midst of them" (Mt. 18:20). Hebrews 13:8 declares, "Jesus Christ the same yesterday, and to-day, and for ever." In the light of the truth of these declarations, for the past 2,000 years people have continued to write books attesting to the works of this *eternal Jesus.*

In like manner, Esther refers to the fact that the Persian chronicles also held additional information regarding Mordecai's deeds. The record of Mordecai's deeds were written in the chronicles of the kings of Media and Persia, and they are a part of the pageantry of the power of this once great empire. The labors of archeology have buried the challenging voices of skeptics by digging up tangible and irrefutable evidence. The majority of this work has taken place within the past 150 years and confirms names and places in Scripture. Possibly, at some point in time, the records that the writer of Esther had at his disposal will be discovered. For the present, however, those Persian records are not available to us. We only have the events the inspired penman extracted to write in the Book of Esther.

Their selection and sequence comprise a spiritual drama that only an eternal, all-knowing God could conceive and produce. Truly, men have received the gifts of knowledge, understanding, and wisdom from God to proclaim the thoughts and purposes of His heart to mankind! Second Timothy 3:16 speaks for itself: "All scripture is given by inspiration of God, and is profitable for doctrine, for reproof, for correction, for instruction in righteousness."

Righteousness Seated on the Throne

Esther 10:3

"For Mordecai the Jew was next unto King Ahasuerus, and great among the Jews, and accepted of the multitude of his brethren, seeking the wealth of his people, and speaking peace to all his seed." As a righteous ruler, he is looking after the welfare of the people and speaking peace.

Every type of historical human government has advocated policies to achieve this same end. However, with the weak, corrupt nature of men on the thrones, we have witnessed only dismal, even atrocious performances. Every type of government has only ruled with its favorites while the rest of the people have paid the dues.

Revelation 11:15 records, "And the seventh angel sounded; and there were great voices in heaven, saying, The kingdoms of this world are become the kingdoms of our Lord, and of His Christ; and He shall reign for ever and ever." Just as Haman's position of power was taken away, so the god of this world, satan (a created fallen being who tried to venture beyond his limitations), shall be replaced by the Lord Jesus Christ.

An awesome view of this ruler is provided in Revelation 19:15–16: "And out of His mouth goeth a sharp sword, that with it He should smite the nations: and He shall rule them with a rod of iron: and He treadeth the winepress of the fierceness and wrath of Almighty God. And He hath on His vesture and on His thigh a name written, KING OF KINGS AND LORD OF LORDS." He will become the sovereign ruler over rulers of nations, the spiritual head over spiritual leaders.

Throughout earth's history, satan has deceived many rulers like Haman into believing that the title, "King of Kings and Lord of Lords," belongs to them. However, this title belongs to the Lord Jesus Christ, for He alone was faithful to the heavenly Sovereign, His heavenly Father. From eternity past to eternity future He has always been the King's Son with matchless qualifications.

These Scriptures clearly reveal what will ultimately transpire, but until that time, this King, Jesus Christ, has been invited to Heaven to take a position until His Eternal Lord achieves His purposes. Psalm 110:1 declares, "The Lord [Jehovah or Eternal One] said unto my Lord [*Adonai* or King], Sit Thou at My right hand until I make Thine enemies Thy footstool."

During the task of neutralizing an enemy, logic and reasoning sometimes bring an end to hostilities. At times, however, chastisement has to be used to bring clear understanding and to separate truth from delusion. As noted in Psalm 110:1, God is at work to fulfill His promise to His Son. He will subdue men by His reason and logic (through His Word) and gain a submission by a confession of faith, or He will subdue them through chastisement and judgments. He will have a subdued and obedient people on earth.

God is truly just and loving, all powerful, ready and waiting to bless a submissive and obedient mankind, Jew and Gentile. All honest and rational people will have no problem surrendering their lives to such a God.

However, this God also has an attribute called holiness. Therefore, He cannot allow sin to come into His Presence. Jesus Christ came first to the nation of Israel as their Savior. The penalty of sin was upon them, even eternal death. Not only on them, but it was on all mankind who had violated Heaven's law. For this Jesus Christ became the Lamb of God who takes away the sin of the world (see Jn. 1:29).

Because He is supreme love and full of grace, He makes this offer to all of mankind. If you perceive that these statements are truthful and you desire to receive this Savior, Jesus, then simply follow the instructions of this Scripture: "But as many as received Him [Jesus the Son], to them gave He [the Holy Spirit] the power to become the sons of God [the Heavenly Father], even to them that believe on His name" (Jn. 1:12). His name is Jesus, *Yeshua* (God is my salvation). Won't you accept His gracious offer today?

The drama of Esther is replete with parallels signifying events and symbolizing characters. These portraits provide insight for our past, present, and future world. What appears to be a complex and intricate story line holds a simple, yet potent plot: a people in need finally recognize their true deliverer and give him the exaltation due him. Have you come to this conclusion?

Bibliography

Abraham, Larry. *Call it Conspiracy.* Seattle, WA: Double A Publications, 1985.

Allen, Gary. *None Dare Call it Conspiracy.* Rossmoor, CA: Concord Press, 1971.

Bordeaux, Michael. *The Gospel's Triumph Over Communism.* Minneapolis, MN: Bethany House, 1991.

Brooke, Tal. *When The World Will Be As One.* Eugene, OR: Harvest House Publishers, 1989.

Church, J.R. *Guardians of the Grail.* Oklahoma City, OK: Prophecy Publications, 1989.

_____. *Hidden Prophecies in the Psalms.* Oklahoma City, OK: Prophecy Publications, 1986.

Cooper, David. *The God of Israel.* Los Angeles, CA: Biblical Research Society, 1945.

_____. *The Seventy Weeks of Daniel.* Los Angeles, CA: Biblical Research Society, 1941.

_____. *Man: His Creation, Fall, Redemption, and Glorification*. Los Angeles, CA: Biblical Research Society, 1948.

Encyclopedia Brittanica. William Benton Publisher Chicago, London, Toronto, Geneva, 1972.

Finegan, Jack. *Myth and Mystery*. Grand Rapids, MI: Baker Book House, 1989.

Gaebelein, Arno Clemens. D.D. *The Conflict of the Ages*. Vienna, VA: The Exhorters Pub., n.d.

Hunt, Dave. *The Seduction of Christianity*. Eugene, OR: Harvest House Publishers, 1985.

Jeremiah, David. *The Handwriting on The Wall*. Dallas, TX: Word Publishers, 1992.

Kah, Gary H. *En Route to Global Occupation*. Lafayette, LA: Huntington House, 1992.

Lockyer, Herbert. *All the Men of the Bible*. Grand Rapids, MI: Zondervan Publishing House, 1985.

Marrs, Tex. *New Age Cults and Religions*. Austin, TX: Living Truth Publishers, 1990.

New International Version. East Brunswick, NJ: International Bible Society. Copyright 1973, 1978, 1984.

Poland, Larry. *The Coming Persecution*. San Bernadino, CA: Here's Life Publishers, 1990.

Price, Walter K. *The Coming Antichrist*. Neptune, NJ: Loizeaux Bros., 1974.

Quigley, Carrol. *Tragedy and Hope.* New York: Macmillan and Co., 1966.

Robertson, Pat. *New World Order.* Dallas, London, Vancouver, and Melbourne: Word Publishers, 1991.

Schenk, Paul. *The Extermination of Christianity.* Lafayette, LA: Huntington House, 1993.

Scofield Reference Bible, King James Version. Westwood, NJ: Barbour and Company, 1968.

Skousen, Cleon. *The Naked Communist.* Salt Lake City, UT: Ensign House, 1961.

Still, William. *New World Order.* Lafayette, LA: Huntington House, 1990.

The Companion Bible, King James Version. Grand Rapids, MI: Kregel Publications, 1990.

White, John Wesley. *Thinking the Unthinkable.* Altamonte Springs, FL: Creation House Publishers, 1992.

Wurmband, Richard. *Marx and Satan.* Westchester, IL: Crossway Books, 1986.

Yamauchi, Edwin M. *Persia and the Bible.* Grand Rapids, MI: Baker Book House Co, 1990.

Zodhiates, Spiros, Th.D. *Hebrew Greek Key Study Bible,* King James Version. Grand Rapids, MI: Baker Book House, 1984.

Frank "Joe" Olsen
369-1446